Windows on the Past: Identifying, Dating, & Preserving Photographs

by

Diane V. Gagel

Published 2000 by

HERITAGE BOOKS, INC.
1540E Pointer Ridge Place
Bowie, Maryland 20716

1-800-398-7709
www.heritagebooks.com

ISBN 0-7884-1620-0

A Complete Catalog Listing Hundreds of Titles
On History, Genealogy, and Americana
Available Free Upon Request

This book is dedicated to my best friend,

my husband

Joseph V. Gagel

Table of Contents

Dating Our Photograph Collections   1

Identifying and Dating: Non-Paper Photographs   5

Identifying and Dating: Paper Photographs   20

Researching the Photographer   30

Dating Costumes 1840-1900   41

     1840-1850   51

     1850-1860   53

     1860-1870   58

     1870-1880   64

     1880-1890   67

     1890-1900   71

Preservation of Our Photographs   75

Using the Photograph Analysis Chart   91

Bibliography   93

Dating Our Photograph Collections

Thirteen years ago I started a new position at the Toledo/Lucas County Public Library as the Photograph Archivist for the Local History Department. During the course of my career there I found a need to compile a list of Toledo area photographers in order to date the photographs in the department's collection. There was a short list compiled by a predecessor, but I found it was not detailed enough for what I had in mind. Therefore, I spent a large part of my time in the first year going through the Toledo City Directories; I also examined the Toledo newspapers page by page for the years prior to the city directories to make my list as complete as possible. I added to this information from other Toledo publications and photographer obituaries. Once I had the information, I then entered it onto my computer as a database. Armed with this information, I could, in some cases, date some of the photographs within a year of being taken. During this time, I learned a great deal about dating photographs as well as the care of the collection.

After I left the Library, I decided that I would compile a list of photographers for the entire state of Ohio up to 1900. I originally intended that the book also contain information about identifying, dating and preserving photographs. However, my publisher wanted to limit the book to the list of Ohio Photographers. (This project was published in 1998 entitled *Ohio Photographers: 1839-1900.*) In the mean time I had begun giving programs around the country at genealogical conferences on dating, identifying and preserving photographs. I then turned to expanding the first part of my original idea and this book is the result. It is my hope that you will find it a worthy addition to your library.

I have inherited a large photograph collection from both of my grandmothers and have added others to my personal collection. Fortunately, both of my grandmothers were alive at the time to name the people in the images and in some cases date the photographs. However, I am well aware that often we find photographs that have vague or no identification. Also many people just enjoy collecting old photographs and would like to know more about their collections. Therefore, I have researched the available current information and, hopefully, have put together an easy but informative manual on identifying and caring for our collections. This is not intended as a technical manual for professionals, but rather as a guide for the typical family or photograph collector. I have tried to include in my list of sources other books of a more technical nature for those who wish to become more proficient in the area of archival preservation.

It is important to remember that in the 19th Century as well as in the 20th Century, photographers copied older formats into the newest format. For example, photographers in the 1860s often advertised that they could make tintypes or cabinet cards of old daguerreotypes or ambrotypes. **So it is important to date not only the type of photograph but also the image itself.** So, what is the procedure for this process? The best way to accurately date photographs involves four stages: 1. Identifying the photographic process; 2. Dating the photographer's years of operation; 3. Identifying and dating the fashions worn in the image; and 4. Dating any props found in the image. Only after coming up with these 3 or 4 dates, can we attempt to approximate a date for a photograph.

1. **Identifying the process.** The first part of the book is divided into two parts: non-paper and paper photographs. In these sections, you will learn about daguerreotypes, ambrotypes, tintypes, carte-de-visites, cabinet cards, etc.

2. **Researching the photographer.** If a photographer is listed on the photograph somewhere this can assist in narrowing down the time span. It is important to check under the image in cased photographs like daguerreotypes, and the backs of paper photographs like cabinet cards. Photographers often had information about their studios or awards they had received printed there. Part 2 then provides information on how to research the photographers found on your photographs. It is also important to request that relatives who are sending you copies of their photographs also copy any photographer information found on the original. Often these helpful relatives think that the image is the only important part. It is, however, only part of the important information found in our collections. So request copies of the entire photograph front and back for card photographs.

3. **Dating Fashions.** In order to date the actual image, we need to date the fashions worn by the individuals in the picture. In my collection, I have examples of several paper photographs that are actually copies of daguerreotypes or ambrotypes. In Part 3 I have presented a brief overview of the 1840s to 1900 of this aspect but you will need to use other fashion sources as well to accurately identify the fashions in the 20th Century as well as find examples of all the fashions available to our ancestors in the 19th Century. This will be the most

difficult part of the research process as most of us are not knowledgeable about fashion trends especially in times long before ours.

4. **Dating Props, etc**. The last area to date includes the furniture or other props found in the photographs. Note any other possible clues these provide. You may have to consult antique furniture books, etc.

Another part of my book concerns **Preservation** of our collections. Again I have taken each of the major photograph formats discussed in the first part of the book and have outlined the current information on preserving each format. Many of our photographs are over a hundred years old and with proper care they can continue to delight the viewer for decades even centuries to come. Since we often want to share our collections or find we want copies from other collections, I have also given an overview of copying old photographs, which does not require you to be a professional photographer. In addition, many of us now use computers and the corresponding hardware like scanners and digital cameras, so I have also included some information on this aspect of image collection. Finally, at the end of my book, I have included a photograph analysis chart that you can use to assist you in this process of dating your photographs

Today, we are fortunate that the archival supplies we need are readily available. It is important to remember the Archivist's motto: **NEVER DO WHAT YOU CANNOT UNDO.** Therefore, before creating a scrapbook or doing anything to your collection, it is important you use archival materials and processes. In addition to my overview, there are many sources on archival procedures and materials if you need more information. Check your local library for other books on preserving your collections.

For my own collection preservation, I have used two archival suppliers. Century Photo Products and Accessories, PO Box 2393, Brea, CA 92822, a division of 20th Century Plastics. (1-800-767-0777 or www.centuryphoto.com). [Note: be sure to purchase only the archival quality products as this company also sells non-archival products.] The other supplier is Light Impressions, PO Box 940, Rochester, NY 14603-0940. (1-800-828-6216 or www.lightimpressionsdirect.com)

I hope you will take the time to identify and preserve those photographs you have collected or inherited. However, do not forget the photographs you have taken. These too need to be properly identified and preserved so that future generations can enjoy them and that they are not lost through ignorance or negligence. Photographs are indeed Windows on the Past for us and for future generations.

STRANGERS IN A BOX
Anonymous

Come, look with me inside this drawer
In this box I've often seen,
At the pictures, black and white,
Faces proud, still, and serene.

I wish I knew the people,
These strangers in the box,
Their names and all their memories,
Are lost among my socks.

I wonder what their lives were like,
How did they spend their days?
What about their special times?
I'll never know their ways.

If only someone had taken time,
To tell, who, what, where, and when,
These faces of my heritage,
Would come alive again.

Could this become the fate,
Of the pictures we take today?
The faces and the memories,
Someday to be passed away?

Take time to save your stories,
Seize the opportunity when it knocks,
Or someday you and yours,
Could be strangers in the box.

Identifying
and
Dating

Non-Paper
Photographs

IDENTIFYING AND DATING HISTORIC PHOTOGRAPHS: NON-PAPER
****
THE DAGUERREOTYPE
1840-1860

The daguerreotype was first introduced in the United States via booklets outlining Louis Daguerre's process in reproducing an image on a silvered copperplate. Many early American daguerreotypists learned through these booklets; however, later ones trained in the studios of the first artists/daguerreotypists like Samuel F. B. Morse. In fact, Morse, along with a chemistry professor John W. Draper, worked on the process to improve the quality and capabilities of the daguerreotype. Daguerre's process could be done only with outside light and involved an exposure time of ten to fifteen minutes. Morse, an accomplished artist, felt this medium would be ideal, with improvements, for portraits; "The daguerreotype is undoubtedly destined to produce a great revolution in art, and we, as artists, should be aware of it and rightly understand its influence."

The first obstacle was the copperplate. Americans began producing higher quality and more highly polished silvered copperplates, which was necessary for clear, acceptable portraits. Secondly, the exposure time had to be lowered. By 1840, the exposure time was cut from the fifteen minutes to mere seconds, thus making it feasible for persons to sit for a daguerreotype portrait. For example, Cleveland daguerreotypist, J. F. Jenkins advertised in 1844 that it took only one and a half minutes to obtain a perfect likeness.

The news of this new process spread very quickly in America. As early as the spring of 1839, some sort of photographic prints was displayed in a Cincinnati bookstore, which were produced by John Locke, professor of chemistry and pharmacy at the Medical College of Ohio. Sign painter Ezekiel C. Hawkins is believed to have established the second daguerreotype gallery in the United States in Cincinnati in 1840. By 1851, Cincinnatians had a choice of thirty-two daguerreotype photographers. They sold $80,000 worth of pictures in 1851. "At the going rate of $5 each for the most popular size, this means 16,000 Cincinnatians sat for portraits in that one year alone." (*The Enquirer*). Four of Daguerre's "Chemical Pictures" were shown at the Cuyahoga County, Ohio, Courthouse on three August evenings in 1842 for the admission price of 50 cents. A letter to the editor extolled this exhibit by saying "a sight of them is worth a score of concerts, or a dozen feats of a grand and lofty tumbling." In an editorial, the newspaper stated that the exhibition was "one of quiet, unalloyed gratification, and the changes produced on the same canvass by different reflections of light are marvels that must be seen to be appreciated or credited." That same fall, the first advertisement appeared in the Cleveland newspapers for a daguerreotype studio, E. Dibble's in the Franklin building.

Many of the better practitioners were accomplished artists, especially of portraiture. As a result, they were experienced in lighting, proportions, and posing. The best results indoors demanded a large skylight or a large window facing northwest. The importance of light in this field is evidenced by the advertisements of early daguerreian galleries. In 1852, the Forest City Daguerreian Rooms of Cleveland announced they had "the largest and best skylight in the city." The next year in the same city, Dr. Crobaugh advertised that his studio had "the largest and most available skylight in the city." By the mid-1850s, daguerreian galleries advertised they could make daguerreotypes in any type of weather.

Daguerreotypists were also proficient in disguising or minimizing flaws of the portrait sitters by placement of the camera. Other techniques included rubbing the skin of a freckled face until it was red in order to disguise the spots. Posing sitters, especially in the early years, reflected the artistic background of the daguerreotypists. The positioning of the sitter, the props, and the backgrounds all were reminiscent of 18th century painting.

It was not uncommon in the early days for a daguerreotypist to have some other occupation, and taking images was a sideline. Cleveland photographer, James F. Ryder wrote in his memoirs that it was common "to find watch repairers, dentists, and other styles of business folk to carry daguerreotype on the side. I have known blacksmiths and cobblers to double up with it, so it was possible to have a horse shod, your boots tapped, a tooth pulled or a likeness taken by the same man; verily, a man--a daguerreotype man, in his time, played many parts."

Daguerreotypes were not inexpensive. A quarter plate, 3.25 inches by 4.25 inches, could cost over four dollars, which was not a small amount in the 1840s. Some of the more well known artists charged five dollars for a daguerreotype portrait. Despite the high price, it was estimated that Americans spent about eight to twelve million dollars annually on daguerreotypes in the 1840s. Obviously, this was a big business.

Many people today remark on the dour expressions found in 19th century photographs. One would think that not a single person in the 1800s ever smiled. However, these expressions were a result of the process, not the personality of the subject. The exposure time for the early daguerreotypes was several minutes in the early years or seconds later in the decades; thus any movement while the photograph was being taken would blur the image. Evidence of this can be seen in photographs of people and their pets, like dogs. The dog is usually blurred, while the people are clear and in focus.

Because of this exposure factor in 19th Century photography, portrait sitters were asked not to smile, for it was impossible to do so for the length of time of the exposure without some movement which would blur the image. Thus the sitter was instructed to maintain a normal facial expression, which could be done without movement, while the plate was exposed. *The Chicago Inter-Ocean* in 1877 carried an article regarding sitting for pictures: If a lady wanted to present a serene expression, she should say "Bosom and keep the expression into which the mouth subsides until the desired effect ...is evident." A distinguished look could be obtained by saying "Brush." If a lady wanted her mouth to appear smaller, then "flip" was the word; larger-- the word was "cabbage"; "Kerchunk" was used for a mournful look, and "Scat" for a look of resignation. Obviously, "cheese" would never do!

In addition, to ensure that the sitter would remain absolutely still, devices were invented like head clamps, the bases of which can often be seen behind or between the subject's feet in photographs. This long exposure time, unfortunately, has resulted in hundreds of photographs of grim-faced ancestors. James F. Ryder, Cleveland daguerreotypist, stated that the daguerreotype camera was "truth itself. What he told me was as gospel. No misrepresentations, no deceits, no equivocations. He saw the world without prejudices; he looked upon humanity with an eye single to justice. What he saw was faithfully reported, exact, and without blemish."

The major characteristic that still set portrait painting a part from daguerreotypes was color. Many daguerreotypists experimented with ways to provide "color portraiture" in a daguerreotype. Some practitioners were also knowledgeable in chemistry, so they experimented with various chemicals which would tint the daguerreotype. This resulted in some having tints of green, brown, or gold. The latter was obtained through gilding the daguerreotype.

However, in 1842 a method of coloring the picture was patented. The daguerreotype was coated with a transparent varnish or gum and then was painted by the daguerreotypist if he or she was an accomplished painter, or by gallery employees whose sole job was to paint over the images. The painting could be of the entire figure, or just simply giving the subject rosy cheeks. Another reason to paint on an image was that the early daguerreotypes were known to fade, so retouching was part of the procedure. Overpainting was also common especially when enlargements were made. This was done in three possible mediums: watercolors, charcoal and crayon.

Many early daguerreotypists were itinerants wandering from town to town with their wagons filled with their equipment and chemicals offering to take pictures of homes, buildings, as well as portraits. These itinerants would stay a month or two in one town and then move on to the next town. A. Bisbee, a Dayton daguerreotypist, wrote an instruction book for his fellow practitioners which detailed what traveling photographers should look for in obtaining rooms for sittings.

> *A traveling artist who can secure an upper room with a window three feet wide and six high, can do very well, but if it be larger it is all the better. A side and sky-light combined make the best light. Each should be about eight feet square, and the sky light should be on an angle of about forty-five degrees. They should always have a northern exposure if possible, or perhaps north-east would be as well.*

In addition to special wagons fitted out to house the photographic equipment, some daguerreians also used the available waterways. Small boats would be outfitted and the daugerreian would float down rivers and stop along the way at farm houses and villages.

In the 1840s, the Daguerreotype business was also considered one of the few suitable places for women to work outside the home . Women were often hired as colorers of photographs and they could earn up to $30.00 a week in the larger cities. Women often ran their own studios as well. An 1863 book on occupations available to women stated that "ladies and children usually prefer a lady artist." Daguerreian studios often employed women in the reception room to receive ladies and other responsibilities in the studio and could earn from $3.00 to $8.00 a week.

Landscape paintings were very popular, so the landscape daguerreotype also found its audience. A popular form of entertainment in the 1850s was the panorama. This naturally led to the use of daguerreian art for panoramas as well. For example, Charles Fontayne and William S. Porter of Cincinnati produced one in 1848, which consisted of eight large-size plates showing the view of two miles of the Ohio River from the town of Fulton to Vine Street in Cincinnati.

Newspapers and magazines also hired daguerreotypists to provide city views and other landscapes which were then copied by engravers to be published. Painters used daguerreotypes of scenes as well. They would copy the image on to canvas and then discard the daguerreotype.

Another popular use of daguerreotypes was for photographing the dead and also for mounting on tombstones. Often one of the first persons called in the event of a death, especially of a child, was the daguerreotypist, so the parents would have a remembrance of the lost child. Some family portraits show a mother or father holding a daguerreotype of a deceased child. If a person had to be buried before a photograph could be obtained, the body may later have been exhumed to be photographed once a photographer was available. J. F. Ryder, a Cleveland, Ohio, photographer, recalled one such incident when he was an itinerant daguerreian in New York. The local blacksmith disapproved of Ryder's occupation, that he was "humbugging and swindling the people of their hard earnings." Ryder moved on to a nearby village and about a week later, he was surprised to see the blacksmith seeking him out. The blacksmith's child had died and he wanted Ryder to return to his village and photograph his dead child.

The daguerreotype was obviously suited for mounting on tombstones in moisture proof cases. A Columbus firm, World Manufacturing Company "offered the Indestructible Patent Aluminum Monumental Photograph Case, made ...of the Wonderful New Metal." One of their advertisements read "Your duty to your beloved friends and relatives remains unfulfilled without having placed one of these beautiful cases upon their monument, so that you and your friends might often see them as they were known on earth."

In another publication, the *Hutching's California Magazine* (May 1857) contained a photographer's advertisement regarding placing daguerreotypes on tombstones:

> *There is often...a feeling of sadness, which falls with gentle stealth upon the heart, when with slow and measured footsteps, we walk among the green hillocks of the dead....If on every tombstone there could be seen the life-likeness of the sleeper, as with sparkling eye, and noble mien he walked 'a man among men'; or of some gentle lady, whose kindly and generous impulses could be read in every feature of the 'face divine'; or of the angel-child, whose joyous laugh, and innocent smile speaks of the loss to its bereaved and loving parents...how much more inviting would then be the last resting places of the departed, could we thus seek the 'living' among the 'dead,' and on every tombstone see the living representative of the sleeper.*

Most American daguerreotypes are found in cases, which usually look like miniature books. It is not known how this developed in this country, but it could be related to miniature painting, which was very popular in the late 1700s and early 1800s. These small portraits were then cased for display and for travel. The early daguerreotypes may have been seen as likely candidates for these cases. Jewel cases were also used in the early days before special daguerreotype cases were manufactured. The early cases were made of wood, paper mache, and later plastic. The right or bottom side of the case was used for the daguerreotype. The daguerreotype was protected by a gold-colored matting and then covered with glass. The three layers were bound together by a protector, which was a thin brass frame which wrapped around the whole. This was then pressed into the frame of the case. The left or top side of the case was padded with silk, satin, or velvet. When closed the case was latched with a small hook.

The daguerreotype ranged in size from 6 ½ x 8 ½ inches to the smallest at 1 3/4 x 1 5/8. The most common size in America was called the "sixth" size: 2 3/4 x 3 1/4 inches. (For more information on the dating of cases, see "Dating Cased Photographs.") It is important to remember, that the date of the case may not be the date of the photograph on the inside, for the daguerreotype cases were often reused for later forms of photography like ambrotypes and even tintypes.

American daguerreotypists entered their works in many forms of art competitions here and in Europe, especially in England. By 1851, American daguerreotypes were deemed of a higher quality than found in England. English critics felt this was due to the cleaner air found in America as compared to London's smoggy atmosphere, which resulted in brighter lighting here than in London. However, part of the difference can also be found in the higher quality of the silvered plates used in America.

However, daguerreotypes were doomed to a short life. By 1860, the daguerreotype was being replaced by less expensive forms of photography: the ambrotype and the ferrotype (tintype). There may have been another factor in its demise. In order to develop a daguerreotype, the plate was immersed in a mercury solution and then heated. Mercury vapor was a by-product of the process, and many daguerreotypists suffered from the effects of mercury poisoning. Whatever the reason, Americans moved on to other forms of photography by the Civil War era.

IDENTIFYING DAGUERREOTYPES

Not all cased photographs are daguerreotypes. It is important to identify the type of photograph in a case before proceeding to date it. There are two simple tests that can be used that do not involve disturbing the photograph. The first one involves the qualities of a daguerreotype. Because the image is produced on a highly polished, silvered copperplate, the image in certain positions will be difficult to see. While holding the cased photograph, move the case around at different angles. If in certain positions, the image seems to disappear, is difficult to discern, or has a mirror-like quality, then it is probably a daguerreotype rather than an ambrotype or tintype. Another test is to use a magnet. Place the magnet at the back of the case section holding the picture. If the magnet is attracted to the case, then it is a daguerreotype and not an ambrotype, which is made of glass; however, it could be a tintype, so the first test should be done as well. In addition, the daguerreotype has a very detailed image when compared to other cased photographs. If you have determined that a cased photograph is a daguerreotype, then it was taken between 1840 and 1860. More precise dating can be done by checking the costumes, etc. found in the photograph.

DAGUERREOTYPE POETRY

"The Old Daguerreotype"
by Eve Wilder McGlasson
June 1892 issue *The Photo-American*

You hev to holt it sidewise
Fer to make the lightness show
'Cuz it's sort uf dim and shifty
Till you git it right.. 'bout so!
An' then the eyes wink at yeh,
An' the mouth is cherry ripe.
Law! It beats your new style picters,
This old digerrytype.

Thar's a blush acrost the dimples
Then burrows in the cheeks;
F'om out them clups o'ringlets
Two litttle small ears peeks.
Thet brooch thet jines her neckgear
Is what they used to wear;
A big gold frame that sprawled around
A lock o' someone's hair.

Twas took 'fore we was married,
Thet there--your maw an' me.
An' times I study on it,
Why, t'fazes me to see
Thet fifty year 'aint teched her
A lick! She's jest the same
She was when Sudie Scriggens
Took Boone C Curds' name.

The hair is mebbe whiter
'An it was in '41
But her cheeks is jest as pinky,
An' her smiles 'ain't slacked up none.
I reckon love--er somethin'--
Yerlunimates her face,
Like the crimsont velvet linin'
Warms up the picter case.

'S I say, these cyard boa'd portraits
They make me sort uh tired,

12

A-grinnin' forf upon yeh
Like their very lips was wired!
Give me the old digerrytype,
Whar the face steals on your sight
Like a dream that comes by nightime
When your supper's actin' right.

****

"The Old Daguerreotype Found by Mrs. Nellie B. Stevens in an old
New Hampshire Attic Trunk"

Up in the attic I found them, locked in the cedar chest,
Where the flowered gowns lie folded, which once were brace as the
best.
And like the queer old jackets, and the waistcoats gay with stripes,
They tell of a worn-out fashion, these old dauguerrotypes
Quaint little folding cases, fastened with tiny hook,
Seemingly made to tempt one to lift the latch and look;
Linings of purple and velvet, odd little frames of gold,
Circling the faded faces brought from the days of old.
Grandpa and Grandma, taken ever so long ago,
Grandma's bonnet a marvel, Grandpa's collar a show;
Mother, a tiny toddler, with rings on her baby's hands
Painted, lest none should notice, in glittering gilded bands.
Aunts and uncles and cousins, a starchy and stiff array,
Lovers and brides, then blooming, but now so wrinkled and gray;
Out through the misty glasses they gaze at me sitting here,
Opening the quaint old cases with a smile that is half a tear.
I will smile no more, little pictures, for heartless it was, in truth,
To drag to the cruel daylight these ghosts of a vanished youth.
Go back to your cedar chamber, your gowns and your lavender,
And dream 'mid their bygone graces, of the wonderful days that
were.

13

THE AMBROTYPE
1851-1880

The development of the ambrotype was the beginning of the end of the daguerreotype, for this form of photography was cheaper than its predecessor. This technique was invented by an Englishman, Frederick Scott Archer. The peak period for this format was in the mid-1850s in the United States. The image is formed on a treated sheet of glass and then backed with a dark, usually black, material. At various times this was black paper, varnish, or velvet. Ambrotypes, since made of glass, were fragile and were housed in casings like the daguerreotype. Later in this period, coral glass, a deep red glass, was used to back the ambrotype, which gave them a rose-colored appearance. Ambrotypes were also hand-painted to add color. A major disadvantage of the ambrotype, besides being glass, is that copies could not be made. Each ambrotype is an original.

IDENTIFICATION OF AMBROTYPES

Most surviving ambrotypes are cased photographs and may be difficult to distinguish from daguerreotypes. However, there are two methods to determine an ambrotype. First, an ambrotype does not have the mirror-like quality of reflecting light like the daguerreotype. Another method to check a cased photograph is by using a magnet. An ambrotype will not attract the magnet since it is made of glass.

DATING CASED PHOTOGRAPHS
1840-1870

An important fact to remember about cased photographs is that the photograph in a case may not be the original one for the case. The case and the photograph should be dated separately. The photograph can be dated by its type: daguerreotype, ambrotype, and tintype. To date the case, the viewer must look at the characteristics of the case.

First, check the mat used to frame the photograph. In the 1840s, the mats were very simple: thin brass mats of oval, octagonal, or other plain designs. A daguerreotype of the 1840s would consist of three elements: the image, the mat, and a cover glass. This was secured in the right side of the case with a rim of velvet-covered cardboard.

In the 1850s, however, a fourth item was added: a pliable gilded brass preserver, which held the three elements together by wrapping around the layers. In the 1850s, the mats are more ornate with scalloped edges perhaps. In the mid-1850s to the 1860s, the mats are the most ornate with beaded edging or embossed designs.

Second, look at the makeup of the case itself. From 1849 to 1854, the cases are book-like and usually made of wood and covered with embossed paper or leather. The designs on the cases would be natural ones. If the case is plastic, then it dates 1854 or later. In the 1860s, the designs on the cases became more patriotic, largely due to the Civil War, so one sees American eagles, Civil War camp scenes, Union Forever motifs on the cases.

In addition, the plastic cases' embossing is more distinct, while the wooden cases often have a softer look to the embossed design. Books on photograph collecting may have illustrations to assist in dating cases.

If you have determined that the cased photograph is an ambrotype and the case is from the 1840s, then the original daguerreotype has been replaced by the ambrotype, which was not available until 1852.

THE TINTYPE OR FERROTYPE
1854-1930s

The ferrotype, or as it is more popularly known, the tintype was invented by an Ohio chemistry professor Hamilton L. Smith of Gambier. Smith had made the first daguerreotype in Cleveland and had experimented with the photographic process while a professor at Kenyon College. With the assistance of a former student Peter Neff, Jr., Smith perfected making an ambrotype on metal, which he patented on February 19, 1856 (patent #14,300). Smith later assigned his rights to the patent to William Neff and Peter Neff, Jr. This became the basis for a business for the Neffs, for they charged a fee for anyone using this process.

The tintype did not gain in popularity until the 1860s, largely due to competing ferrotype firms, like that of another Ohioan Victor Griswold, who held his own patent for the process using a thinner sheet of metal. The Civil War made the tintype the most popular form of photography because of its durability, unlike the ambrotype, and its quick development time--one minute from exposure to finished product. With the appearance of the tintype, the Civil War soldier could carry a photograph of his loved ones without fear of breakage as in the ambrotype. In addition, if he had his photograph taken on the battlefield or in camp by one of the many traveling photographers in the battle zones, he could safely send the tintype home to his family.

IDENTIFICATION

A tintype is easy to identify since it is done on metal, a thin sheet of black jappaned iron which was coated with a collodion wet plate emulsion. The resulting image was a reversed positive one. Another factor that aided the tintype's popularity was the development of the multi-lens camera, which could take multiple images on a single metal sheet. After being processed the sheet was cut apart leaving pictures usually 2 ½ x 3 ½ inches. However, it was also possible to make very tiny portraits for buttons, campaign pins, etc., with 36 images on a 5 x 7 metal sheet.

Early tintypes were often put in old daguerreotype or ambrotype cases. It is often difficult to distinguish between cased ambrotypes and tintypes. The easiest way is the magnet test. However, most tintypes are not found in cases, but loose or in photo albums. To establish a date can be difficult because of the long period in which they were made. If the image has a chocolate-brown tone to it, it dates after 1870. However, to be more precise in dating it, the viewer must look at other aspects of the tintype's image: the props and the fashions. (See other sections for information on these aspects of dating photographs.)

On the top left, we can see how the cased photograph is arranged. First, the daguerreotype or ambrotype is covered by the glass. Then the matte is placed over the glass. Finally, the three pieces are held together by the preserver. Once all is assembled, then the image is placed in the case.

Above you see the daguerreotype once all the elements have been combined and has been replaced into the case.

The above is an example of an ambrotype, which as one can see is a negative image. On the right is the backing which is used to make the image a positive.

When the black backing is acquired, the image is now clearly visible. In this example we can see the markings left by the case which housed the ambrotype.

The tintype below illustrates one of the problems faced by all of us who have tintypes in our collections. The image often has become quite dark. This may have been the way it was originally, or time and exposure to the atmosphere may have darkened the image. Making a black and white negative using slow speed film may lighten it. Also using scanners and modern photograph editing software could also lighten and enhance the image for re-copying on a negative.

Identifying and Dating

Paper Photographs

IDENTIFYING PAPER PHOTOGRAPHY:
1854-1900 AND 20TH CENTURY
****
ALBUMEN AND SALT PRINTS

The next major step in the history of photography was the development of the albumen print, which was made on pure rag stock. The stock was treated with the protein obtained from egg whites and then sensitized. The resulting prints were then mounted on boards. This process dominated photography from the 1850s to the 1890s.

In this form of photography, the egg whites were added to a salt solution, then beaten to a froth to break down the various proteins. Then the mixture was left to age for a week, which often resulted in a distinctive aroma in the albumen manufacturing facilities. There were some side effects of the albumen process; the diet of the hens changed the properties of the print. For example, some prints turned yellow and faded; therefore, citric acid was added to preserve the print, but then they had a tendency to turn the prints brown. (Many photographers wondered what to do with all the leftover yolks, so a photography journal at the time ran a recipe for "Photographer's Cheesecake.")

Salt prints were also made during this time period. This process was simpler and cheaper, but the picture quality was poorer than albumen because the fiber and texture of the paper was visible.

To determine the type of print, hold the print up horizontally to the light. If the surface appears glossy, then it is probably an albumen print. Deterioration of the albumen print results in a sepia tone to the image. Salt prints exhibit a dull finish when held to reflect the light, and the image color is sepia, brown, or even purple. The prints, salt or albumen, were then mounted on cardstock to provide stability and strength.

The two most common formats of card photography are **carte-de-visites** and **cabinet cards.**

CARTE-DE-VISITE
The carte-de-visite was first made in the late 1850s and is the size of a calling card of the time, hence the name. The picture measures 2.25 x 3.75 and is mounted on a paper support measuring 2.5 x 4.

The earliest prints, 1860-68, can be dated by the stock and other details. The mounting paper will be thin with square corners, and be of white or ivory tone. The area surrounding the picture will have border lines, usually double lines, the outer one thicker than the inner line. These border lines may be gold, black, red, or light purple. The border may also consist of a single line. Often the image is done in an oval framed vignette. The picture may be hand colored. If there are any props in the image, they will be very simple: columns, a chair, or balustrades.

If the reverse of a carte-de-visite has a tax stamp (looks like a postage stamp), this photograph was made between September 1, 1864 and August 1, 1866. These revenue stamps were required on paper products to provide revenue for the Civil War costs. The denomination of the stamp is an indication of how much the taxed product cost: 2 cent stamp, less than $.25; 3 cent stamp, $.25- $.50; 5 cent stamp, $.50 - $1.00. For products costing more than $1.00, then there would be a 5 cent stamp for each additional dollar value.

Carte-de-visites of the 1870s were on heavier stock, a medium weight, rounded corners, and were white, cream or beige. The front of the card may be white, while the reverse of the card may be colored (pink, dark green) or may have a pattern of some sort. These cards have only a single border line of red, gold, black or purple. The props were more fanciful: bridges, fences, perhaps a fake rock.

From 1880 to 1905, carte-de-visites' mounting boards were thick with rounded corners. The mounts were white, cream, light green, or even pink. They may have a single border line, but may not have any border; however, the card stock may have gold beveled edges. One popular technique was the photo montage: an oval portrait surrounded by an actual photograph of a forest, for example. In the image itself, elaborate backdrops may be found, such as an outdoor scene.

CABINET CARDS

This larger mounted photograph dates from 1869, but the heaviest production was from 1880-1906. The photograph is 3.75 x 5.5 inches mounted on a board measuring 4.25 x 6.5 inches. The mounting board and decoration on the board can assist in dating these cards. In the 1870s, the stock was thin with square corners and white or cream. The border consists of a single colored line. There may be some limited advertising on the reverse, but is usually plain. Colored mounts of deep brown or maroon with gold printing can also be found in this period.

The cabinets of the 1880s are thicker with rounded corners. The mounting stock is usually tinted as well: gray with double green borderlines; tan with single brown line; cream with brown printing; black with gold edging; gray front with a pale yellow reverse. There may also be colored printing on the front with a single line of some design.

In the 1890s, the cabinet stock became more colorful: rose, primrose, maroon, bottle-green, pale green, beige with gold-beveled edges, or a gold serrated edge. On the reverse, there will be elaborate advertising.

After 1900, the mounts become plainer, usually gray with colored printing. The surface of the card may be pebbled or have an embossed edge design. The image may be surrounded by a scalloped framing.

One may find other size photographs applied to cardboard other than the above mentioned carte-de-visite and cabinet. In 1870 the Victoria Card was introduced. This measures 3 1/4 x 5. In 1875, the 4 x 7 Promenade was developed. Soon after one could buy other sizes, usually for framing: Boudoir, 5 1/4 x 8 ½ ; the Imperial, 6 7/8 x 9 7/8; and the Panel Card, 8 1/4 x 4.

STEREOGRAPHS

Stereographs were first produced in the 1850s. Most of these were of commercial subjects, not family pictures. Many of us may have inherited these mounted photographs and their viewers, or find collecting these a fascinating hobby. To date these photographs, the mounting can be helpful.

    1851-1867-- mountings have square corners, are flat and made of thin stock.

    1868-- the mounting boards have rounded corners.

    After 1879-- the mount is curved or appears to be warped.

The color of the mounting board can also give some idea of the time period.

    1851-1862--the mount colors were white, gray, ivory, cream, brown, pale-blue, green, or lavender. From 1860-63, the cards were dull gray, flat with square corners.

    1862-1872--the colors included light to dark yellow.

    1865-70-- the colors were purple, pink, violet, red, green, and blue.

    After 1877-- the colors included beige, tan, dark-gray, black, orange and yellow.

    1893– the card is gray, curved with rounded corners.

    1902-- A black mounting, curved with rounded corners.

For more details on stereographs, consult John Waldsmith's *Stereo Views: An Illustrated History and Price Guide.*

OTHER FORMS OF PAPER PHOTOGRAPHS

Two other types of paper photographs that may be found in family collections are **Woodburytypes** and **cyanotypes** These may not be mounted on cardboard, but may be found in scrapbooks or loose in photograph collections. Woodburytypes were made from 1865 to the 1890s. These can be easily identified by the image's reddish tint. The cyanotype's (1885 to 1910) tint may range from blue to even violet.

The image will be very sharp in both of these types of photographs. Copies of these can be made by using the appropriate colored filter which will result in a very sharp black and white copy.

DATING CARD PHOTOGRAPHS

It is important to remember that dating the type of photograph does not necessarily date the image. Early photographers often advertised that they could make copies of daguerreotypes and ambrotypes.

Therefore, the card photograph you may have in your collection may actually be a copy of a photo taken 10 or 20 years earlier. As a result, you should also date the fashions worn by the persons in the image. If the fashions correspond to the dates of the photograph medium, you will know the approximate date of the image.

Also if a photographer is listed on the card, then you should also verify his/her period of business. If all three dates then correspond, then you have properly dated the photograph.

OVERPAINTING, COLORING, AND OTHER TOUCH UP PROCESSES

From the very beginning of photography the biggest drawback was the lack of color. Miniature portraits, the predecessor of the daguerreotype, may have been affordable only to the wealthier customers, but it did have color. When the daguerreotype appeared on the scene, the lack of color was seen as a problem in making the new art form popular despite the lower costs of such a medium. Daguerreotypists and later photographers all experimented with developing color photography, but failed until the 20th Century. However, to make up for this, most if not all studios offered various forms of overpainting or coloring to their patrons.

Gilt was added to jewelry worn by the sitter, or added even if the sitter had worn no gold jewelry. Rosy cheeks might be added to the daguerreotype image. This was also done with the ambrotype and tintype. Another factor that may have required some type of "painting" was that improperly processed or stored daguerreotype would begin to fade. Therefore, some studios offered to paint over the fading image to bring it back to its original image.

Studios often employed trained portrait painters to "color" their daguerreotypes, ambrotypes, etc. Often the early daguerreians and photographers were former portraits painters and thus often legitimately called themselves "artists." In addition, women found employment in this field to add color to the finished image.

The next stage in altering the image was retouching the negatives for card or paper photographs. This was first developed in Europe in the

23

1850s, but it is not believed to have been widely used in the United States until after the Civil War. The larger format of the cabinet card emphasized any personal defects of the sitters. These defects of either the actual sitter or the resulting negatives could now be "retouched" on the negative to improve the resulting image.

An instruction book on *The Art of Retouching* by Burrows & Colton and Ourdan in 1880 commented on the real purpose behind altering the actual image on the negatives: "The most difficult subjects are persons who insist upon being *taken just as they are*. Negatives of such may be flattered with impunity, as it usually turns out that they do not wish to be represented *just as they are.*"

Other forms of enhancing a photograph, specifically paper ones, were later used by studios. For example, many of us have large pictures that appear to be charcoal or ink portraits. Enlarged photographs were done on plain paper and sometimes the resulting enlargement was not very satisfactory. So the artists employed in the studios would overwork the image in charcoal, India ink, or watercolor.

Enlargements were also done on other mediums beside paper and then over painted in some form with charcoal, ink, oil paints, etc. In photography studio advertisements, we find such things as ivorytypes. Other hard mediums were ceramic, enamel and milk glass. In the 1880s, a process was developed to enlarge a photograph onto canvas which was then finished by an artist in some other medium. This also meant that old daguerreotypes, ambrotypes, etc., could be transferred to a canvas to be painted. Therefore, to date the image use the same techniques as with dating any form of photographic image.

A good source to aid in understanding and dating the type of "retouched" or colored photograph in your collection is *The Painted Photograph 1839-1914: Origins, Techniques, Aspirations* by Heinz K. Henisch and Bridget A. Henisch.

20th CENTURY PHOTOGRAPHS

One of the most common early 20th Century photograph in family collections is the photograph postcard. These were especially popular before World War I. One clue that might be helpful is that divided backs, that is one side for address another for a message was not allowed in the United States until 1907. If the back is divided, then the postcard was produced 1907 or after. If the postcard is not stamped and canceled or there is no date recorded on message area, then the image will have to be dated by the costumes.

Many excellent resources are available in libraries and bookstores to date early 20th Century fashions.

The 20th Century also saw the rise of the amateur photographer with the availability of the Kodak cameras. The early ones were similar in concept to our throwaway versions today. The first Kodak cameras came loaded with film. When the roll was finished, the camera owner would mail the camera to Kodak who would then develop and print the film and then reload the camera and return to the owner. This later changed to the familiar concept of taking them to a photograph developing studio like we do today.

However, once the amateur could take photographs, the family picture collection changed.. The photographs were still in black and white, but now we find more candid shots in the collection rather than the posed studio shots of the previous century. We also often find negatives of various sizes in our collection. These pre-World War II negatives need special attention (See Negative Storage section).

Hopefully, these 20th Century photographs have been identified, but as with early forms, photographs were often thrown in boxes, or put in albums without identification. So, these photographs need to be identified and dated as best as possible. Since there will be no photographer's name, one needs to check the clues found in the picture itself. Furniture, houses, cars (especially license plates and car models), and clothing can all provide clues to the date of the image.

Although photographic film was not overly expensive, people did not waste film. They often reserved picture taking to important family events: marriages, christenings, Golden wedding anniversaries, holidays, etc. Also if a relative or close friend came for a visit, these were often commemorated with photographs. Thus we often find photographs of people on the front porch or lawn (no flash in the early years).

If you know some of the people in the picture, perhaps you can estimate the date by their probable age at the time of the picture. Also family diaries and letters in our collections may provide clues as to when a photograph was taken. Compare the undated photograph with ones that have been dated/identified. Are there any similarities? Clothing? Furniture?

Newspapers may also provide clues. I have in my collection a large photograph of the Brown Family Reunion in Preble County, Ohio. Reunions were often noted in newspaper columns in the late summer and early autumn. I found a notice in the county newspaper about the reunion and that a photograph was taken!

If you have any living relatives of an age to have been around when a picture was taken, ask them to give you some advice about when the picture would have been taken and where. In the process you may hear some fascinating family stories.

After World War II, prints were often dated on the margins. In the latter part of the 20th Century, prints are often dated on the back.

Don't overlook any clue, no matter how minute, when dating 20th Century photographs.

The chart below may assist you in dating some of the 20th Century color photographs in your collection.

Kodachrome	1935
Kodacolor	1941
Ansco-Color	1942
Ektachrome	1943
Ektacolor	1947
Polaroid	1948
Kodachrome II	1961
Polacolor &	
Instamatic	1963
SX-70	1973
Kodachrome 25 &	
Ektachrome 64	1974
Numbers replace	
names on Kodak film	1976

Also check slides and prints for dates that may have been stamped on them when processed. This is the date of processing and may narrow a time frame.

E. V. Ellis, Photographer,
ALLIANCE, OHIO.

CABINET CARD

SHOWN   ACTUAL SIZE

OF 4.25" X 6.5"

CARTE-DE-VISITE SHOWN

ACTUAL SIZE OF 2.5" X 4"

This 20th Century Photograph can be dated not only by the costumes, but also by the prop—the automobile. This was taken at a county fair. The gentleman is my grandfather, Harry Kinninger, and his friend is Rose Siegel.

Researching

The

Photographer

RESEARCHING A PHOTOGRAPHER

An important factor in dating a particular image is the photographer. Knowing when the photographer and his/her studio was in operation can help us date when a photograph was made. However, it is important to remember that the photograph in question could also be a copy of an early format, so use all the variables when dating a photograph. If the photographer is known, then we have one more date to put into the equation.

On the very earliest forms of photography, like the daguerreotype, ambrotype, and tintype, there may not be any photographer's name found. For those situations, the researcher will have to rely on the photographic medium and the costumes to date the image. However, beginning with the carte-de-visite and the cabinet cards, the photographer had the opportunity to put his/her name and studio address on either the front or reverse of the cardstock.

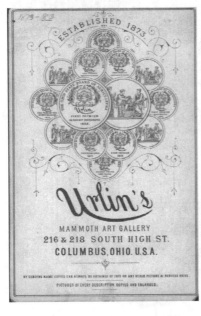

The reverse of a photograph may have dates, like this one on the left, which gives the dates of awards won by the photographer; the most recent one is 1883.

If a photograph does have the studio/photographer's name attached, the researcher now has a third date element, but researching a photographer's period of operation at a specific address can be very time consuming unless a local or statewide listing has been compiled. So where does a researcher begin in compiling a history of a studio's period operation?

LOCAL/STATEWIDE COMPILATIONS

Before beginning any lengthy search, go to a library with access to a computerized statewide catalog search or OCLC (a nationwide listing of library materials). Once at the library catalog computer, search on subject headings such as "Photographers." Then limit the search by "Photographers--Arizona" for example. If you are interested in just one local region, try "Photographers--Phoenix, Arizona." If there is anything in print, it should come up on the catalog screen. If this has failed to locate a published listing, then contact the state's historical society or library. One can also try a county or city library or historical society to ascertain if the local institution has compiled their own list of photographers. [See the listing at the end of this chapter for possible sources of photographer lists in each state.]

PERSONAL RESEARCH

If no list can be found, then the researcher will have to do the legwork. What follows is a list of sources that may yield information on photographers and their years in business. The sources are listed by ease of research, i.e. time spent vs. information obtained.

Census Records: Beginning in 1850 the U. S. Federal Census listed occupation of adults. The drawback to the using the census records is that 1. it was taken every 10 years and many photographers may have gone into and out of business during that gap between census years; and 2. Sometimes the term artist is used instead of photographer. One can use the census records from 1850-1920 at the current time. Many states have indexed their census records, so the researcher can quickly determine if the photographer is listed in a particular census

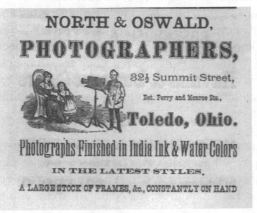

Business and City Directories: Beginning in the mid-19th Century many states have state-wide directories of businesses in operation. They are usually divided by type of operation, i.e. daguerreotypists (for the early years) or photographers (beginning about 1860). Then the

31

address and/or location (town/city) is listed. These may not be found every year, but enough years may be located to provide a good list of dates. There are also regional directories or county directories of a similar content. Most large cities also have a long run of directories. These directories generally have a separate business section again divided by type of business. Also check these directories for display advertisements by the photographers which may provide additional information about the studios.

City Promotional Publications: Many cities or publishing companies in cities compiled business profile publications which served to promote the business community in that city. These appeared often in the late 19th century--the period of big business--and contain detailed histories of various industries and businesses like major photographic studios.

County and Town Histories: Most counties in the late 19th century published county histories. These often contained lists of businesses in towns and cities at the time of publication. Also check the biographical sections for the name of the photographer you are seeking. These contain family information but often include a brief history of the individual's beginnings in the business.

Newspapers: Nineteenth Century photographers advertised in newspapers just as they do today. However, searching newspapers can be very time consuming. Most old newspapers are on microfilm and are unindexed; therefore, a researcher will have to do a daily search perhaps through many years of newspapers, so before beginning such a search, narrow the dates as much as possible through other sources.
Notwithstanding, during the Great Depression, the WPA abstracted and indexed by subject many city newspapers. These are usually available on microfiche at the city library. If your city's newspapers have been abstracted/indexed by the WPA, this will shorten your research time enormously. Also check with the local librarians for obituary indices they may have compiled. Photographers' obituaries often give time frames for periods of business.

Tax Records: State and Local Tax records may include information on businesses, like photography studios. However, another major source would be the Federal Occupational Tax passed in 1862 which took effect on August 1, 1862. These are available from the National Archives and provide the person's name, occupation, and location. The inclusion of photographers in this taxation was repealed in 1870. The Federal Occupational Tax records are part of the records of the Internal Revenue Service in the Civil Reference Branch.

National Photographers' Press: Once photography became a popular occupation and widespread, national photography publications began. These publications may contain lists of photographers or subscriber lists. Also photographers often wrote to these publications, in the form of letters or articles which may mention period of operation. Unfortunately, finding or gaining access to these may be difficult as they may be housed in their original format in very few locations or only found on microfilm. Again check with your local library on where these publications can be found.

Photographers' Associations: Photographers, like many businessmen and/or artists, liked to meet with their fellow practitioners. Therefore, they formed organizations, usually on a statewide level, in order to learn about new procedures and generally discuss the "business" or "art" of photography. Check to see if your state of interest still has such an organization and how far back their records may go. Also check with state historical societies for the records of defunct associations. The associations may have also published anniversary histories which may be found in libraries.

STONE'S PHOTO. & COPYING HOUSE. POTSDAM, N.Y.
FINELY EQUIPPED. A LARGE CORPS OF SKILLED ARTISTS. HEADQUARTERS OF INTELLIGENT PHOTOGRAPHY.
INDIA INK PORTRAITS, COPYING AND ENLARGING, BOTH AT RETAIL AND FOR OTHER PHOTOGRAPHERS,
AND AGENTS AT WHOLESALE.

Current Published Photographer Directories or Contacts

ALABAMA
[No Statewide Listing published]

ALASKA
[No Statewide Listing published]

ARIZONA
Rowe, Jeremy. *Photographers in Arizona, 1850-1920: A History and Directory.* Nevada City, CA: Carl Mautz Publishing, 1997.

ARKANSAS
[No Statewide Listing published]

CALIFORNIA
[No Statewide directory published, but major metropolitan areas have been compiled.]

Palmquist, Peter. "California Nineteenth Century Women Photographers." *The Photographic Collector* Vol. 1, #3 (Fall 1980): 18-21.

Palmquist, Peter E. *Shadowcatchers I: A Directory of Women in California Photography before 1901.* Arcata, CA: Peter E. Palmquist, 1990.

COLORADO
Harber, Opal. *Photographers and the Colorado Scene, 1853-1900.* Denver: Western History Dept., Denver Public Library, 1961.

CONNECTICUT
Fuller, Sue Elizabeth. "Checklist of Connecticut Photographers by Town: 1839-1889"
"Alphabetical Index of Connecticut Photographers: 1839-1889." *The Connecticut Historical Society Bulletin,* Vol. 47 #4 (Winter 1982): 117-163.
Contact: Greg Drake, 47 Wiltshire Rd., Brighton, MA 02135.

DELAWARE
[No Statewide listing published]

Current Published Photographer Directories or Contacts

DISTRICT OF COLUMBIA
[No comprehensive list published]
Contact Paula Fleming, National Anthropological Archives,
Smithsonian Institution, Room 60-A, Natural History Building,
Washington, D. C. 20560.

FLORIDA
[No Statewide listing published]
Contact: Richard Punnett, 111 Coquina Ave, Ormond Beach, Florida
32174-3303.

GEORGIA
[No Statewide listing published]
Contact: Lee Elsroth, George Department of Archives and History,
330 Capitol Ave, Atlanta, GA 30334-1801.

HAWAII
[No Statewide listing published]
Contact: Lynn Davis, Chairperson; Visual Collection, Bernice P.
Bishop Museum, PO Box 19000A, Honolulu, Hawaii 96817

IDAHO
Hart, Arthur A. *Camera Eye on Idaho: Pioneer Photography 1863-
1913.* Caldwell, Idaho: The Caxton Printers, Ltd, 1990.

ILLINOIS
Czach, Marie. *A Directory of Early Illinois   Photographers.*
Macomb, IL: Western Illinois U., 1977.

*Chicago Photographers 1847-1900 as Listed in Chicago City
Directories.* Chicago: Print Department, Chicago Historical
Society, 1958.

Contact: Jim Foster, PO Box 3008, Urbana, IL 61801.

INDIANA
[No Statewide Listing published]
Contact: James Marusek, Ore Branch Rd., PO Box 442, Bloomfield,
IN 47424-9018.

Current Published Photographer Directories or Contacts

IOWA
[No Statewide listing published]
Contact: Iowa State Historical Dept., State Historical Society of Iowa, 402 Iowa Ave., Iowa City, IA 52240.

KANSAS
[No Statewide listing published]

KENTUCKY
[No Statewide listing published]

LOUISIANA
[No Statewide listing published]

MAINE
[No Statewide listing published]
Contact: Greg Drake, 47 Wiltshire Rd., Brighton, MA 02135.

MARYLAND
Kelbaugh, Ross J. *Directory of Maryland Photographers 1839-1900.* Baltimore, MD: Historic Graphics, 1988.
Kelbaugh, Ross J. *Supplemental Directory of Baltimore Daguerreotypists.* Baltimore, MD: Historic Graphics, 1989.

MASSACHUSETTS
A Directory of Massachusetts Photographers, 1839-1900. Camden, ME: Picton, 1993.
Polito, Ronald, compiler. *A Directory of Boston Photographers: 1840-1900.* 1983, rev. 1985. Available from Dept of Art, U. of Massachusetts-Boston, Harbor Campus, Boston, MA 02125.

Also contact Polito at same address for directory of Massachusetts photographers in 19th Century.

Current Published Photographer Directories or Contacts

MICHIGAN
[No Statewide listing published]
Contact: Thomas Ross, 35892 Parkdale, Livonia, MI 48150
or
David Tinder, 6404 Coleman, Dearborn, MI 48126.

MINNESOTA
[No Statewide listing published]
Contact: Publications and Research Division, Minnesota Historical
Society, 690 Cedar St., St. Paul, MN 55101.

MISSISSIPPI
[No Statewide listing published]

MISSOURI
[No Statewide listing published

MONTANA
[No Statewide listing published]
Contact: Montana Historical Society, 225 N. Roberts St., Helena, MT
59601.

NEBRASKA
[No Statewide listing published]

NEVADA
[No Statewide Listing published]

NEW HAMPSHIRE
[No Statewide Listing published]
Contact: Greg Drake, 47 Wiltshire Rd., Brighton, MA 02135.

NEW JERSEY
[No Statewide listing published]
Contact: New Jersey Institute of Technology, Newark, NJ 07102

NEW MEXICO
Rudisill, Richard. *Photographers of the New Mexico Territory 1854-
1912*. Santa Fe: Museum of New Mexico, 1973.

NEW YORK
[No Statewide listing published]
Torok, George D. *Hidden Years: Early Photography in Western New York.* NY: Buffalo State College, 1993.

NORTH CAROLINA
[No Statewide listing published]
Contact: Photographic Services Section, CB #3934, Wilson Library, U of NC, Chapel Hill, NC 27599-3934.

NORTH DAKOTA
[No Statewide listing published]
Contact: Frank E. Vyzralek, Great Plains Research, 702 Capitol Ave., Bismarck, ND 58501.
Also The Dakota Image, 636 West 21st St., Sioux Falls, SD 57105

OHIO
Gagel, Diane V. *Ohio Photographers, 1839-1900.* Nevada City, CA: Carl Mautz Publishing, 1998.

OKLAHOMA
[No Statewide listing published]
Contact: Photograph Archivist, Oklahoma Historical Society, Wiley Post Historical Building, Oklahoma City, OK 73102.

OREGON
Robinson, Thomas. *Oregon Photographers: Biographical History and Directory, 1852-1917.* Portland, OR: Thomas Robinson, 1993 (Revised).
Contact: Oregon Historical Society Photographs Library, Oregon Historical Society, 1230 S. W. Park Ave., Portland, OR 97205.

PENNSYLVANIA
Ries, Linda and Jay W. Ruby. *Directory of Pennsylvania Photographers, 1839-1900.* Harrisburg: Pennsylvania Historical and Museum Commission, 2000.
Other Contact: The Center for Visual Communication, PO Box 128, Mifflintown, PA 17059.

RHODE ISLAND
[No Statewide listing published]
Contact: Greg Drake, 47 Wiltshire Rd., Brighton, MA 02135.

SOUTH CAROLINA
[No Statewide listing published]

SOUTH DAKOTA
[No Statewide listing published]
Contact: The Dakota Image, 636 West 21st St., Sioux Falls, SD
57105

TENNESSEE
[No Statewide listing published]

TEXAS
Haynes, David. *Catching Shadows: a directory of 19th Century Texas
    Photographers.* Austin: Texas State Historical Association,
    1993.
Or
Contact: David Haynes, Institute of Texan Cultures, U. Of Texas, PO
Box 1220, San Antonio, TX 78294.

UTAH
[No Statewide listing published]

Carter, Kate B., compiler. *Early Pioneer Photographers.* Salt Lake
    City: Daughters of Utah Pioneers, 1975.

VERMONT
[No Statewide listing published]
Contact: Greg Drake, 47 Wiltshire Rd., Brighton, MA 02135.

VIRGINIA
Ginsberg, Louis. *Photographers in Virginia 1839-1900: A Check List.*
    Petersburg, VA: Louis Ginsberg, 1986.

WASHINGTON
[No Statewide listing published]

WEST VIRGINIA
[No Statewide Listing published]

[WESTERN STATES]
Mautz, Carl. *Biographies of Western Photographers: A Reference Guide to Photographers working in the 19th Century American West.* Nevada City, CA: Carl Mautz Publishing, 1997.

WISCONSIN
[No Statewide Listing published]

WYOMING
[No Statewide listing published]
Contact: Loren Jost, 308 Moose Dr., Riverton, WY 82501.

NATIONAL LISTINGS

John Craig. *Craig's Daguerreian Registry.* 2 vols. Torrington, CT: John S. Craig, 1996.

Bruce Baryla, c/o Ciociola & Co., 888 Seventh Ave., NY, NY 10106.

Directory of Civil War Photographers. Contact: Ross J. Kelbaugh, Historic Graphics, 7023 Deerfield Rd., Baltimore, MD 21208

Willis-Thomas, Deborah. *Black Photographers, 1840-1940: An Illustrated Bio-Bibliography.* New York: Garland, 1985.

CANADA

Contact: Joan M. Schwartz, Chief; Photography Acquisitions & Research, Historical Resources Branch, National Archives of Canada, 395 Wellington St., Ottawa, Ontario, K1A ON3 Canada.

Mattison, David. *Camera Workers: The British Columbia Photographers Directory, 1858-1900.* Victoria, Canada: Camera Workers, 1985.

Dating

Costumes

1840-1900

DATING PHOTOGRAPHS THROUGH COSTUMES 1840-1900

****

Since many forms of 19th Century photography covered so many years, it is often difficult to pinpoint the time period of the individual photograph. In addition, card photographic copies were often made of daguerreotypes and ambrotypes many years after the original had been made. Therefore, if the form of the photograph and the name of photographer is unknown or undateable, then the costume may be the only remaining factor.

The items to be aware of are the changing fashions for men and women, the hairstyles, and accessories for each sex and for children. For women, the details to check are the hairstyle, bonnets (type and where worn on head), sleeve styles, skirt styles, and bodice styles. Girls' dresses were often miniature versions of their mothers' styles. For men, check carefully the cravat, especially width and style; coat lapels (width and cut); vests, pant styles, and hats either worn or shown in the picture. Facial hair or lack of it can also help determine the date. The type of facial hair, like the muttonchop whiskers, also can be helpful.

1840-1850

The 1840s began with little fanfare; however, many changes were to come about in the world and in the United States. At the beginning of the decade, a queen named Victoria married her Albert and marked the beginning of the Victorian era. In the U. S., War of 1812 hero, William Henry Harrison is elected president, and the first emigrant train to

41

Oregon travels through Indian territory. By mid-decade relations between Mexico and the U. S. have deteriorated, which will result in an armed conflict and the addition of Texas and other formerly Mexican territories to the United States. Famine is spreading in Europe and hits Ireland particularly hard. Thousands of Irish and other European emigrants come to the New World. By the end of the decade Europe is plagued with one revolution or rebellion after another. The end of the decade also saw gold in California, the first railroads being built, and another cholera epidemic in many parts of the United States.

Fashion in the 1840s was not static either. As the decade progressed, the clothing styles were modified, although not as dramatically as the political lines of the decade.

In the early 1840s, women's dresses had a long-pointed bodice with a full dome-shaped, floor length skirt. The shoulders may be dropped and sloped with long, tight sleeves. Collars may consist of dainty lace. Accessories were parasols and fingerless black gloves.

Women's hairstyles were very simple: parted in the center and pulled severely back into a bun or covered with a bonnet. The hair covered the ears. The bonnets were worn on the back of the head rather than on top or towards the front as found later in the century.

In the late 1840s, the sleeves became wider, the bodices were shorter and not as pointed. The skirts were adorned with flounces.

Girls' fashions were copies of their mothers, but with shorter skirts and pantalettes visible beneath the skirts. Girls' hair was also parted in the center like their mothers. Pre-teen girls often had their hair cropped short to just above the shoulders. Teenage girls usually allowed their hair to grow to eventually be worn up like their mothers.

Men's fashions consisted of dark frock coats and trousers which had no cuffs and no crease. Hats were very tall top hats. The waistcoats were the only variety: figured and brightly colored. The men's collars were high and stiff and worn with cravats, which were wrapped and tied.

A man's hair was always parted on the side and curled forward over the ears. Sideburns were present and beards were worn, but below the chin.

Young boys wore dresses like their sisters until the age of four or five, but their hair was always parted on the side. Thus if you have difficulty determining if a child in a dress is male or female, look at the part in the hair. Center part = girl; side part = boy.

Older boys work ankle length pants that buttoned to the shirt; they often wore short, simple jackets.

1850-1860

The 1850s did not begin very auspiciously for the United States. President Taylor dies in office and Congress attempts to calm the waters between northern and southern states. Irish emigration reaches its peak in 1852. Railroad expansion continues unabated, while only half of the American population is involved in farming. The decade ends with another gold strike in the Rockies and John Brown's raid at Harper's Ferry.

Just as the nation is moving slowly toward conflict, the fashions of the 1850s start to see the changes that will become the trademarks of the Civil War era..

This decade saw the beginning of the hoop skirts. The skirts also had three or four flounces but could have as many as twenty-four flounces. The bodices were less elongated and the sleeves were shorter and wider with tiers. The collars were often trimmed with a brooch. Women's bonnets were smaller and worn further back on the head.

Girls' dresses had shorter skirts and pantalettes and the material was often plaid or checked.

Men's fashions were similar to the previous decade, but there were some distinguishing features that can be found. Frock coats and top hats can still be found, but the coats, waistcoats and trousers usually matched. The coats are shorter than the 1840s, double-breasted, and looser. Coat collars and lapels decreased in size, and often only the top button was fastened.

Instead of the top hats, men wore straw, low-crowned hats with wide brims. Turned down collars became the fashion, while the cravats were more elaborate and bow ties appear. Men often wore fancy vests. Full beards were now fashionable for men.

Boys' fashions became more distinctive with Zouave or bolero jackets. They wore plaid stockings and low boots. Boys' costumes often were trimmed with braid or tassels.

1860-1870

With Lincoln's election in 1860, the differences between the free and slave states no longer could be compromised. The war dominated the first half of the decade. Upheaval is still occurring in Europe; Garibaldi's insurrection in Italy also inspired fashion styles. Reconstruction in the South causes social and political turmoil in the United States. The end of the Civil War also brought about changes in fashion.

Hoops were still very much in evidence in the 1860s; however, the flounces disappeared, for the skirts were plain or trimmed in geometric patterns. Women's sleeves now were bishop sleeves--full but gathered at the wrist. Women often wore separate jackets, which were short and the dresses were ankle-length.

Women's fashions changed after the Civil War. Their dresses became more elaborate with ruffles, pleats, scallops, fringes and buttons. Some skirts had trains, but hoops were smaller and now had overskirts. Sashes were a popular accessory.

Hats were smaller and worn on top of the head. If no hat was worn, the women have more elaborate hairstyles, including using hair pieces to augment the styles. Curls were also found on the foreheads.

Girls' fashions now included the Garibaldi skirt worn with a full skirt with a wide band of contrasting color near the hem.

There were little changes in men's clothing. The suits had matching pants, and the coat was boxier with no waist seam, and sleeves were bulky compared to the previous decades. Trousers were often plaid or checked. Shirt collars were turned down with narrow bow ties. Beards were more common for men during this decade.

Boys often wore a shirt with knee-length Garibaldi pants, and stockings were horizontally striped. Caps reflected a military theme. Shoes were usually boots.

1870-1880

The 1870s is one of relative calm for the United States. Americans begin to tire of the ongoing problems in the South and Reconstruction ends by the end of the decade. The decade is the beginning of what became known as the Gilded Age. The industrial might of America has replaced England in the world markets. Many financiers saw the beginning of their wealth in this decade. The fashions reflected this changing attitude in America.

The big change in women's fashions in the 1870s was the bustle. The dresses were short-waisted, bouffant style with a draped overskirt and a train. The dresses may be decorated with pleats, bows, buttons, ruffles, ribbons, and fringe. The colors were more vivid, and the hats were now quite small.

Women's hair fashions now involved pulling the hair back into a snood or chignon, or topped by plump braids or a fringe of curly bangs.

Women's accessories became more elaborate: fringed cravat bows or lacy jabots at the throat, velvet neck ribbons, heavy gold chains, jet necklaces, crosses, pendant earrings, fans, and elaborate parasols.

There were a few minor changes in the last part of the decade: the bustle became smaller and the dresses had more of a princess line. The hats were higher in the crown and heavily decorated.

Girls' dresses had ruffles and overskirts. Large bows in the back and decorative aprons were now fashionable for young girls. The hair was shoulder length and bangs were popular.

Men often wore a sack coat over a matching suit often made of textured material. The lapels were wider and longer. Hats were now bowlers or straw. Overcoats were usually Chesterfields with velvet collars. Men's hair was shorter, beards were less common, and moustaches were more prevalent.

Boys were knickers, or below the knee pants, and side-buttoned tunics and wore short hair like their fathers.

1880-1890

The 1880s saw much of the same in America as the 1870s. Industry continued its dominance of the economic and political life of the country. Most of the conflicts with the Native Americans had been resolved either by force or by treaty. Cities and wealth were growing. The fashions of the day reflected the continuing prosperity of most Americans. Many were also buying the new Kodak camera to take their own pictures.

The 1880s saw the arrival of the corset in women's fashion. The look involved extremely fitted basque bodices, tiny waists, and trim hemlines. The dresses included intricate draping and trimming on the skirts. Sleeves were shorter than previously. The bodices may be composed of material that was asymmetrical in patterns.

In 1882, the bustles returned briefly. Accessories were still parasols, fans, and umbrellas. Hats, however, became more elaborate; the hats were moderate in size with high crowns and were decorated with flowers, berries, feathers, plumes, bird wings, or even entire birds.

For girls and young boys, dresses were straight and low waisted and decorated with pleats, scallops, ruffles, or shirring. Striped stockings were still in vogue. Older girls often wore smaller versions of their mothers' styles.

Four coat styles were common for men in this decade: sack coat, frock coat, four-button cutaway, and a dress coat. Collars were buttoned high at the neck and lapels were smaller. Men's clothing fit tighter than previously. Trousers were checked or solid, but did not match coats.

For hats, men still wore bowlers, but also boaters and caps were now in fashion. One major change was in the hairstyles--men now sometimes parted their hair in the center.   Boys during the 1880s wore knee length pants until the age of 12; then they wore long pants like their fathers.

1890-1900

The last decade of the 19th Century saw some distinctive changes. Restrictions on women in the work world were loosening, which was reflected in more practical clothes for women. Men and women were also participating in sport activities like cycling, which meant that clothing had to adapt to a more active population, both male and female. Society is seeing the results of expanded educational opportunities for both sexes--more publications, more jobs for the educated, and more possibilities to move up the economic ladder.

One of the major changes in women's fashions in the 1890s was the adaptation of some male fashions to women's styles. For example, women now wore separate skirt and shirt waists which had a more tailored look and accessories now included bow ties and masculine four-in-hand cravats. Women even wore straw boaters similar to the men's.

The more feminine dresses had narrow skirts, which were often gathered and draped. Sleeves were becoming fuller to eventually the very full Leg-o-Mutton in the late 1890s.

Hats were larger, generally heaped with bows, flowers, lace, ribbons, feathers and birds.

In the late 1890s epaulets and exaggerated wide collars became fashionable; skirts became narrower and very slim. Bodices were decorated with lace.

Women's hair was worn up and off the forehead. The epitome of the look for the 1890s was the Gibson girl.

For young girls, dresses and coats often had some cape effect at shoulders.

Men wore sack suits in the 1890s. The collars were moderately broad, and lapels were winged or turned down. For sports events, men wore knickerbocker pants. Ties were now a staple of men's fashions, with the four-in-hand being the most common.

The homburg joined the derbys, bowlers, and straw boaters.

For boys, there were some significant additions. For very young children, the dresses were longer. For boys, the hair was worn longer and curled. Striped stockings were becoming part of the past and stockings were now usually solid, dark colors. Wide, soft scarves were tied in bows and worn with decorated trouser and jacket outfits. Two of the most popular outfits for young boys were sailor suits and the Lord Fauntleroy look.

The graphics found in this chapter will be of assistance in identifying the costume styles found in your own photographs. However, for more examples of the costumes found in the bibliography at the end of this book.

PROPS USED IN PHOTOGRAPHS

The props used in 19th Century photographs reflect the development of the art and the trends of the period. Early photographs are often devoid of any props, being merely head shots. However, as the century and the skill progressed, so did the use of props.

Photographs in the 1860s will have very austere props like a balustrade, a column, or just a curtain.

The 1870s brought a little romance into the scene with perhaps a rustic bridge and stile.

By the 1880s, photographers had numerous props made especially for their studios like a swing that never moved, a hammock, or fake railway carriages.

The 1890s brought more exotic props: palm trees, cockatoos, and the biggest fad for men and women--the bicycle. Backdrops became more elaborate as the century progressed. The early ones were very plain; later ones could put the sitter in Egypt, Siberia, or any other exotic locale. The furniture used could also be a clue to the date of the photograph. Compare the furniture in the pictures to a book on furniture styles.

When trying to ascertain the date of a photograph use all the

47

elements available to you: the type of photograph, the photographer's period of operation, the fashions, and the props. Alone or in combination, these elements should provide enough information to obtain a fairly accurate date for any photograph.

WHAT TO LOOK FOR WHEN ANALYZING FASHIONS OF MEN AND WOMEN

‹‹ Hairstyle: does hair cover ears, types of curls if any. Hat stylesand placement: is hat on back of head, on top of head, etc.

‹‹ Bodice area: type of collar; any jewelry; sleeves' length, width ,style; waistline: natural, pointed, dropped waist.

‹‹ Skirt: hoop, slim or close fitting, bustle, length of skirt.

‹‹ Do not forget the props (or lack of props) in the photograph may also help date image as well.

Note the differences in the dresses worn in the photograph above and this photograph. Note also the more elaborate background and props in this as compared to the one above.

◄◄ Note the hairstyle: length of hair, part, and facial hair, if any.

◄◄ Check collar style and cravat or tie style

◄◄ Check size of lapel as this varied throughout the decades.

◄◄ Width of sleeves if visible

◄◄ Double-breasted or single-breasted coats.

Note the difference in the lapel size in this photograph

This man is wearing a much different coat style than the man above.

When the pants are visible, note the material or pattern of the pants as well as the width of the pants' legs. These all varied throughout the decades.

1840-1850

1840-1850

This 1840 picture shows some of the characteristics of women's hair and clothing fashions. Women's hairstyles were very simple and pulled back over the ears. The high collared dress with a narrow lace adornment. Other clues include the simple setting. Note also that this image was once in a case as we can see the oval marking left by the matting in the case.

The lady on the right illustrates the most common hairstyle for women during the 1840s, which was parted in the middle and pulled back covering the ears.

The lithograph on the left shows how the women wore their hats in this decade. It was worn on the back of the head with the brim framing the face.

This 1846 N. Currier print shows the typical male wide lapel coat with an extravagant tie which extends beyond the lapels of the coat.

The woman's hairstyle is another option of the 1840s with ringlets extending from just above the ears to the shoulder. The dress has the tight V-shaped bodice with a fuller skirt.

This image from a daguerreotype of a little girl shows the center part used only by girls and the cropped hair. The child is wearing a long jacket over a dress which cannot be clearly seen.

This image also shows the hand of probably the mother who is sitting next to the little girl, but the photographer has scratched off the image of the mother or woman next to the girl.

1850-1860

(Aquilla Whitacre, taken c1852 probably in Preble County, Ohio, about the time of his marriage to Sarah Brown VanSkiver.)

1850-1860
Women's Fashions

This drawing from 1851 shows the changes about to take place in the upcoming decade. The hoop skirt is hinted at in these Americanized French fashions. The parasol is also a popular accessory. Notice the bodice's pointed effect has been shortened from the previous decade. However, the hairstyle is still very similar to the 1840s–parted in the middle and swept back over the ears.

Note the hair is still swept over the ears and also notice the lace hair covering often worn by married women when in public. This woman's dress has the dropped shoulders with high lace collar adornment. The sleeves are fuller than in the 1840s.

When viewing photographs in albums, carefully remove the photograph to check for other clues. This tintype, found in an 1880s album, clearly shows this is a copy of a daguerreotype. Note the nails holding the daguerreotype so the photographer can copy it and the oval markings denoting the original had been in a case. Therefore, the image is from the 1850s.

This is an enlarged copy of an earlier photograph probably from an ambrotype taken in the 1850s.

Note the man's chin line or saucer beard. His hairstyle includes the hair brushed down over the ears but swept up on the top. The tie is not as flamboyant as in the 1840s, but the coat lapels are still wide. However, the vest lapels have a curved or rounded effect rather than the sharper edged lapels.

Note the woman's hairstyle. Also she has the wider sleeves and the tight, boned bodice. Also note the lace collar. The skirt is wider but not yet using the hoops of the next decade.

(D. Harris Copying House, Tyrone, PA)

This is an ambrotype taken sometime in the 1850s. These kind of shoulder or bust shots are often difficult to date. But the cravat and the lapel widths can be useful in dating the costume in addition to the photograph medium of the original. Also note the stand up collar under the cravat.

(Ambrotype of William Kelly, Preble County, Ohio, c 1855)

These two children are wearing clothing that was very typical in mid-19th Century. Note the striped stockings on both children. The child on the left is obviously a boy denoted not only by his clothing but also the side part of the hair. The child on the right is a little girl as her hair is parted in the middle and combed behind her ears.

This little boy is wearing a very popular mode of stocking found in the 1850s and 1860s, the striped stocking. Children often wore plaid stockings in this same period. The patterns did not necessarily match that of the clothing.

This print from an 1850s Ladies Magazine shows the various styles of clothing worn by children at various ages. Older girls worn dresses that were very similar to their mothers'. Younger girls often wore the lace trimmed pantalets as seen on the girls in the upper part of the drawing. (*Godey's Lady's Book*, Vol. XLV, 1852.)

This engraving shows the two types of dresses worn in the 1850s. The woman on the left is still wearing a dress wuth a relatively plain skirt. The woman on the right is wearing the more popular flounced skirted dress. One can see the growing popularity of the hoop skirt when comparing the two ladies. Notice also the ends of the sleeves are wider and shorter which reveals the fancy undersleeves. Note also how the hat is worn further back on the head and tied with a bowed ribbon. (*Godey's Lady's Book*, Vol. XLV, 1852.)

1860-1870

1860-1870

In this drawing from *Harper's New Monthly Magazine*, we have the ideal dress style for April 1861 for women and a child's pardessus. It would appear very grand and most of the women and children we see in photographs would not be dressed this grandly. However, we do see the elements of the 1860s: the wider skirt which will soon incorporate the hoop, fuller sleeves, and a more natural waistline. The hair covering of lace or ribbon is also seen here and in photographs, especially for married women.

The photograph on the right shows the more typical example of 1860 women's dress. Notice the apparent hoop skirt, natural waist often belted, and the fuller sleeves. Also note the similarities of the hair style between this photograph and the drawing above.

This drawing, also from *Harper's New Monthly Magazine,* shows the types of outer clothing women wore over the hooped dresses. Notice also that the hats are now worn forward or on top of the head as the hair is not gathered in the back of the head rather than on top.

In the photograph at the left we can see how the cloak in the above drawing was transformed for the average woman in America. Note also the parasol used to keep off the rain as well as protect a woman's skin from sunburn.

This photograph shows a typical posing of a couple, perhaps for a wedding picture. The woman's dress has the natural belted waistline, fuller sleeves, and hooped skirt.

The man is wearing a vested suit. Notice the much narrower lapels on both the suit and the vest. The turn down collar is also a change from earlier decades as well as the smaller cravat. Also, we often see baggier pant legs in the 1860s than we did previously.

(Carte de visite taken by J. W. Hutton, West Salem, Ohio.)

This simple photograph shows the average man in the 1860s. Samuel VanSkiver was a farmer in Preble County, Ohio, a former Quaker who had migrated from New Jersey as a child to Ohio. Nevertheless, we can see the 1860s characteristics of men's clothing: narrow lapel, bow tie cravat, vest, baggy pants not of same pattern/material as coat and vest. The boots are a working man's boots.

This family grouping of twin sisters and probably their husbands and children, shows a little fancier dress, perhaps their Sunday best or even the wedding suits for the men. We also see examples of the styles for boys and girls. Note the similar style of the women's dresses differing only by the sleeve decoration.

The little boy is wearing a round cut jacket popular at the time. The little girl's outfit is typical with a looser collar than her mother's dress, and she is wearing pantelets. It appears that her hair has been cropped, which young girls wore until they were old enough to care for their own hair.

(From the Preble County Historical Society, Eaton, Ohio, collection.)

When we can find full length photographs of men it is much easier to date the clothing. This man is wearing the double breasted frock coat with velvet collar. The vest has a shawl collar. Note the baggier trousers. Also at this time, most men combed their hair back from the face and over their ears, rather than covering their ears.

(Carte de visite taken by W. P. Egbert, Davenport, Iowa.)

The above photograph shows the variety of clothing styles worn by men and women in the 1860s, some were probably from older siblings or kept and worn for a period of years. The women in the front row are wearing the fingerless lace gloves worn in the 1860s.

Although Children's clothing can be difficult to date, one can attempt to do so by using the same clues as for adults at the time. Children's clothing reflected their adult counterparts, both male and female. The hoop skirt on the girl to the left reflects women's fashions. Also use the doll as a clue by checking doll history resources.

The photograph taken in the mid-1860s shows the traditional cropped hair parted in the middle for little girls. The dress also shows that children's clothes were often just miniatures of their parents' styles. The natural waistline with a full skirt, although girl's skirts were shorter to allow for better, safer movement.

(Mary VanSkiver, d/o John Brown VanSkiver and Sarah Parker, b. 29 July 1857, Israel Twp., Preble County, Ohio.)

This photograph of first cousins Clara and Elizabeth VanSkiver was taken about 1869 in Preble County, Ohio. It shows the shorter dresses worn by younger children. One can also see the pantalettes worn under the dresses. Notice the girls also have the cropped hair but the hair has been curled into ringlets.

(On the left: Clara B. VanSkiver, d/o of Joseph G. VanSkiver and Rebecca Ritchie, was born 12 Aug 1866. Her cousin on the right is Elizabeth May VanSkiver, d/o John B. VanSkiver and Sarah Parker, born 19 Jan 1866.)

1870-1880

1870-1880

The 1870s saw the development of the bustle and the tighter profile for women in their clothing. Notice in the drawing at the left how much has changed in the skirt. Instead of the hoop skirt which disguised a woman's hips we now have form hugging skirts. The bustle first appeared in the early 1870s. It disappeared or was smaller by the end of the 1870s but then reappeared in the mid-1880s. The dresses often have high necked bodices, the bodice covers part of the hips, and tighter sleeves. The dress on the left is actually three parts: the basque (bodice) top, the overskirt which forms the bustle effect, and the underskirt.

Other areas to check are the hairstyles; fringed bangs are common along with one or more than one corkscrew curls brought forward over the shoulder of the woman. Jewelry is more evident as well. Hats are worn on top and forward on the head.

This photograph shows the more elaborate collar treatments found in the 1870s on women's dresses. Note the brooch and necklace.

This woman is also wearing one of the popular hairstyles, the corkscrew curls. In this case she is wearing three over her shoulder. Hair pieces were available for women who either did not have enough hair for the latest style or did not want to style their own hair into those curls.
(Photograph by North & Oswald Art Studio 45 Hall Block, Toledo, Ohio.)

The photograph on the right shows a more common hairstyle of the decade: the fringed bangs. The high collar with lace is also more common for everyday wear.

(Photographer: Rank Bros., Photographers, Van Wert, Ohio.)

This bridal photograph was taken in the late 1870s. If we compare the dress here to those of the 1860s, we can see the huge difference in style. Notice the gathers in the front of the skirt. Also note how much fancier the whole outfit is compared to previous decades. Despite the elaborate bridal veil, one can still detect the fringed bangs.

The man's formal attire also shows some changes. The overcoat has tighter sleeves and the pants legs are narrower. Also note the turned down collar on the man's shirt. [The base of the head brace stand can be seen behind the man's ankles.]

Note the changes in the tie/cravat from earlier decades. Also notice the collars is turned down over the cravat/tie area. The vest has shawl collar and the coat lapel has a rounded edge rather than the sharper ones of previous styles.

Photograph of Willard E. Eldredge, born 24 September 1857 and died 3 April 1873.

(Photographer: Powelson's Opera House Gallery, 223 Jefferson Ave., Detroit, Michigan.)

Children's fashions sometimes are difficult to date. Girls' fashions are often miniatures of their mothers' styles. Therefore, girls in the 1860s wore hoop skirts, although much shorter than their mothers' skirts. In the 1870s girls dresses reflected the tighter form of their mothers' but shorter and not as confining.

Boys' fashions were also a reflection of their fathers'. Lapels, jackets, and pants were similar to the men's fashions. Below we have a young man still in short pants, so he is probably under the age of 12. Note the head brace stand which can be seen between the boy's legs.

1880-1890

William and Lavinia Moore and children: Back row L-R: Silas
Moore, Mary Moore Felton, Lurton Felton, and Martha Moore
Taylor. Front Row L-R: Amie Arkill Moore, William Moore, Lavinia
Bowman Moore, and Thomas Taylor.

1880-1890

The 1880s saw the return of the bustle. However, the front of the dress was to be very straight with an almost unnatural profile to the woman's figure. Stylish women during this time period often had their photographs taken with a side angle of various degrees to show off their bustle. Note the fringed bangs are still in fashion.

(Photographer: S. C. Urlin Mammoth Art Gallery, 216 & 218 South High St., Columbus, Ohio. Taken about 1884.)

Note the fringed and curled hair. Polonaise jacket over the skirt now extends well below the hips with black beading trim along hem.
Also note high lace collar with fichu. Bustle is just visible on the back of the dress. Underskirt has pleated ruffles along the hemline. Note the more elaborate backdrop and balustrade than found in earlier photographs.

(Identified on reverse as "Grandma Remsberg." Photographer: Van Sickle, Springfield, Ohio.)

Fringed bangs with rest of hair piled on top of head.
Basque bodice with high lace collar
Note jewelry and watch chain.
Straight lined front over pleated over skirt and underskirt with ruffles. Bustle is more pronounced in this photograph.
Furniture in photograph can be used to date photographs as well.

(Photographer: H. W. Immke, Princeton, Illinois.)

WOMAN: Draped skirt with hint of bustle. Bodice with high neck and button down front.
CHILDREN: Smaller versions of mother's dress. Lace collar on the girls' dresses.
MAN: Checked suit with narrow lapels. Moustache is more prevalent in 1880s than previously. Narrow pants legs.

This man is wearing a very typical four button cutaway jacket. It was fashionable in this decade to button just the top button. Note the narrow lapels, the watch chain, and bow tie with high collared shirt. Note also that the pants material does not match the coat's. Props have become more elaborate as well.

(Photographer: Lawson & Hill, 40 & 42 East Main St., Springfield, Ohio)

This photograph illustrates three of the styles of clothing that children wore. From the hairstyles, it appears these are
two girls and the youngest is a boy. The girls' skirts are knee length with dark hose. Each child is wearing the lace collars popular in the decade for children. The girls also have the fringed bangs.

(Photographer: F. Smith Art Studio, Van Wert, Ohio.)

This little boy is wearing the popular outfit of the 1880s for young boys: a Lord Fauntleroy velvet jacket and skirt with the wide lace collar.

(Photographer: J. M. Strode, Railroad Street, Kokomo, Indiana.)

This young girl shows a fashionable dress for the older child. Her skirt has two rows pleated flounces. She also has a lace collar and lace sleeve decoration. The heavy chain necklace is very common in this period. Note how her hairstyle is similar to the women.

(Identified as Theresa M. Lappin, New Philadelphia, Ohio. Photographer: S. K. Krauss, Lima, Ohio.)

This photograph illustrates another type of suit coat worn by men in the 1880s. In this case all four buttons were closed. Note the narrower sleeves on the coat. Also note the shorter hair worn by men in this decade. The moustache appears again.

(Photographer: Rank Bros. Photographic Studios, Van Wert, Ohio.)

1890-1900

1890-1900

This family portrait contains several different examples of late 1890s fashion. For the women, look for the leg-o-mutton sleeves. In addition, two of the young women are wearing the new shirtwaist dresses that were fashionable especially for young women who worked outside the home. Men's fashions show how narrow the lapels had become and the bow tie. Also note that now a young man could wear a center part. (Photographer: A. J. Spahr, Deshler, Ohio.)

This portrait of a young woman shows another style of dress with the narrower sleeves from the early 1890s. Notice the shortened bodice and the pleated skirt. Other clues in the photograph are the furniture. Note the corsage and the scroll. By the 1890s more women were graduating from high school and this was commemorated then as to day with a special trip to the photographer. White was often worn for graduation exercises.
(Photographer: McKecknie & Oswald, 619 St. Clair St., Toledo, Ohio.)

This photograph of a little boy illustrates the very popular Little Lord Fauntelroy outfit for boys in the 1890s. Also note the straw hat, which was a popular style for men and boys in this decade. The boy is also wearing knee pants and high button shoes. Although in the 1890s some boys may have their hair parted in the middle, most still followed the traditional side part.

(Photographer: Campbell's Art Studio, No 7 E. Main St., Van Wert, Ohio.)

These boys are wearing a modified outfit for the older boys. It still has the wide white collars and bows, but the coats are more like their father's type of suit coat. These boys are still in their short pants, which gives some clues as to their ages. Note also the high button shoes.

(Photographer: McKecknie & Oswald, 619 St. Clair St., Toledo, Ohio)

When dating photographs, do not overlook the props found in the photograph, such as chairs, tables, and in this case a baby carriage. The wicker baby carriage is the epitome of the 1890s.

(Photograph of Thomas Marshall Bennett, born 1 Aug 1893 in Silver Creek, New York, taken when he was 3 months old. Thomas died on 18 December 1898 in Silver Creek. Photographer: N. S. Chase, Silver Creek, New York.)

72

These young men, Clyde Vick and George Fauble, are sporting a very popular outfit known as the three piece lounge suit. These included the vest, buttoned completely, and four pockets on the coat. The striped pants, shown here in two styles, was also very popular. Another feature to note is the four-in-hand tie and winged collars.

(Photographer: E. V. Ellis, Alliance, Ohio.)

The most obvious way to date this image is the mutton chop whiskers, very popular in the 1890s, although most were not to this extreme. This man's frock coat and vest appear to be very expensive. He is also wearing what appears to be a diamond stickpin. (Photographer: North & Oswald, Toledo, Ohio.)

The fashion items to check on this young man's outfit is the frock coat with medium width lapels. Also note the high buttoned vest and the turned down collar on the shirt. One of the biggest clues in this photograph is the bowler hat, which were worn by men and boys in the 1890s. If the man is wearing any jewelry like a watch chain or a pin, use a loupe to magnify for details. This man's watch fob appears to contain the head of a deer or elk.
(Photographer: J. J. Ream, 7 S. Washington, Van Wert, Ohio)

73

This fashion plate from the 1890s shows the exaggerated bodice and waistline that fashionable women were forced to endure. Note the leg-o-mutton sleeves atop the tight sleeve. Another item of interest is the hat. Hats were worn on top of the head and were often lavishly adorned with flowers and feathers, even entire birds.

(From *Harper's Bazar*, 22 August 1896)

The bucolic scene below shows the casual wear of the times. Note the straw hats worn by the women. Two men's styles are shown form the time. The man in the middle has a more familiar tie, while the young man in the background is wearing a cap and a bow tie with one button closure on his jacket. (*Harper's Bazar*, 22 Aug 1896)

Preservation

of

Our

Photographs

PRESERVATION OF OUR FAMILY
PHOTOGRAPH COLLECTIONS

CARE OF DAGUERREOTYPES

Cased Daguerreotypes usually have survived with little problems through the years even if stored in adverse conditions. However, removing a daguerreotype from its case can be extremely harmful if not done properly. It should not be cleaned except by a professional, and even then more harm than good could be done. The most that should be done by an amateur is to clean the cover glass with distilled water and a mild soap, and then rinsed in distilled water.

If you are thinking about having the daguerreotype cleaned, then the person should be qualified to archivally handle historic photographs. Some daguerreotypes' images are indistinct due to tarnish on the copper plate. This can be removed or lessened by a wash first in distilled water and a mild soap and then in a solution of thiourea, phosphoric acid, and nonionic wetting agent. The plate would then be rinsed in distilled water and, then to prevent water spots, rinsed with ethyl alcohol. The plate will have to be thoroughly and carefully dried. This should not be attempted by an unqualified individual. However, if you are taking a daguerreotype to someone to have it cleaned, inquire how they will be doing the cleaning. If you have any doubts about their procedures, get a second opinion before subjecting the plate to a cleaning..

Daguerreotypes should be archivally stored in a dry, cool area and not exposed to chemical fumes. The ideal conditions are about 66 degrees F and 30 to 40 % humidity. Acid-free containers should be used. To preserve the image, a copy of the daguerreotype should be made on black and white film. Copies can then be shared with family or displayed.

CARE OF AMBROTYPES

If the ambrotype image is distinct or clear, little needs to be done to the ambrotype. The non-emulsion side of the glass can be cleaned with a clean dry cloth, if needed. However, if the image is marred is some way, it may be due to the black backing of the plate. A new backing can make a world of difference in the quality of the image.

However, before attempting to do any type of restoration, have a photographic copy made of the image. Once that is done, one can proceed to provide a new backing. Remove the ambrotype in its preserver frame from the casing. Carefully remove the frame, and set aside the ambrotype--emulsion side up.

DO NOT ATTEMPT TO CLEAN THE EMULSION SIDE OF THE GLASS. The original form of backing may be a black varnish. Do not attempt to duplicate this. If parts of the varnish has begun to flake or the paper or cloth backing has deteriorated to the level to mar the image, then a backing replacement can be done.

The best form of replacement backing is a piece of polyester-based sheet film. This film should be one that has been fully exposed to light and then developed and archivally washed. This would need to be prepared in advance of replacing the backing to ensure the new backing is completely dry. Cut the film to fit the back of the ambrotype, and then restore the preserver frame to the glass plate. Place the film in the case first, followed by the ambrotype. You should now have a greatly improved image.

Before reinserting the ambrotype in the case, check for any information that may be in the case, such as photographers' names, etc. Once this has been recorded, then replace the ambrotype in its case. Storage would be the same as cased daguerreotypes: 60-70 degrees F, 30-40% humidity

CARE AND STORAGE OF TINTYPES

Tintypes can be cleaned with a mild soap solution and then rinsed with distilled water. Since a tintype is metal and subject to rust, it should be thoroughly and carefully dried from a distance with a hair dryer on the low heat setting. Although durable, tintypes do show signs of wear and abuse, like creases and scratches. Nothing can be done to restore the original image. However, professional photographers can eliminate many of these problems through retouching, etc. and provide a very good copy. With the use of scanners and photographic programs, the image can be improved. Once the tintype image has been improved, then a photographic copy on black and white film should be made to preserve the improved image.

The best way to store tintypes is in polyethylene sleeves, similar to the ones used for negative storage. This will protect the image and allow easy viewing. Storage conditions are the same as for other types of photographs.

CARE AND STORAGE OF CARD PHOTOGRAPHS

Historic photographs should not be displayed. If you wish to display historic images, like pictures of ancestors, it is recommended that only photographic copies be displayed. The originals should be stored in archival conditions: cool, dark, and dry.

Some photographic supply companies now have archival quality photograph albums, some similar to antique photograph albums. Paper photographs can also be stored in mylarTM sleeves. However, if this is not done, then store photographs in acid-free archival paper envelopes. These can then be kept in archival boxes or in metal cabinets with baked enamel finishes. Photographs should never be stored in wooden cabinets as wood contains acid which can migrate to the photographs.

Historic photographs (or any photograph) should NEVER be kept in what is known as magnetic albums. These albums are very acidic and have glue-like substances than can eventually destroy the photographs.

Never store photographs near household chemicals, like paint or other chemicals emitting fumes. These can react with the photographic chemicals in historic photographs.

Photographs found in 19th Century albums should be checked for discoloration due to contact with the album pages. If this is found, the photographs should be removed and stored archivally, noting the arrangement of photographs in the original album as this may lead to clues to dating or identifying persons in the pictures.

Of course, the best way to preserve any historic photograph is to have a negative made, archivally store the original and the new negative, and use only the copies made from the negative. With the availability of archival albums that have the appearance of 19th Century albums, older prints or copies of older prints can be displayed in a manner like they were originally.

Proper storage environment is important, as well. Humidity should be maintained between 30 and 50 percent. Temperatures should be between 50 and 77 degrees Fahrenheit. Ideally the temperature should be below 68 degrees F. For color film, the ideal temperature is 50 degrees F.

The storage area should be as free as possible from air contaminants. Metal cabinets or shelves are the best place to store photographic archival containers. Prints should be stored in the dark, especially avoiding ultra-violet light from sunlight or fluorescent lights.

An example of an adequate storage area that can be found in the average home would be in a closet with metal shelving or in an air-conditioned room free from any household chemicals, like paint, cleaning fluids, etc.

Fire-proof safes of various sizes are also available and the historic family albums or photographs can be stored in them as well as long as the above environmental conditions are maintained.

CARE AND STORAGE OF 20TH CENTURY PRINTS

As stated before, do not use magnetic albums. Today many companies offer archivally safe storage sleeves for any type of photograph. Also available are archivally safe scrapbooks with acid-free pages and adhesive materials.

NEGATIVE AND PRINT STORAGE

Many of us have hundreds of **negatives,** old and new. We tend to treat these less importantly than we do the prints. However, the negative is the most important part of photography preservation, for these are the sources of the prints we display and share.

When handling negatives and prints it is important not to touch the emulsion side of a negative or the print's surface, for the acid in our body will affect the negative and the print. The best procedure is to use cotton gloves when handling negatives and prints, especially historic photos.

If there should be a fire or flood or even a lesser form of tragedy, the prints can always be replaced if we take proper care of our negatives. Storage of negatives is similar to the above regarding temperature (66degrees F, colder for color), humidity (30-50%; 15-30% for color), and avoid exposure to chemical and other fumes.

If negatives have become dirty, they can be cleaned with film cleaner. Prints and negatives that may have grease, adhesive (from tape), pen and pencil marks can be cleaned with a product known as PEC-12© which will clean the emulsion archivally and leaves no residue. If there is surface dirt on prints, this can best be removed by a material known as groomstick. Wallpaper cleaner can also be used on prints, but never on negatives or non-paper photographs.

Slides that have been damaged or have fungus should have the cases removed and destroyed; the film transparency should be cleaned and then re-cased in new slide sleeves. Fungus can be avoided by storing the slides in low temperatures and humidity.

Glass negatives pose a special problem due to their fragility. Archival paper envelopes should be used to encase each plate. These then can be stored vertically in archival boxes. NEVER STORE GLASS PLATES HORIZONTALLY. Any pressure on glass plates stored horizontally may break the glass and possibly destroy the image.

Film negatives should be placed in archival negative sleeves, which can be purchased for any size of film. These sleeves can be easily labeled for later retrieval to make duplicates. If possible, color negatives should be stored at a lower temperature and humidity (15-30%) than B & W. This will slow the rate of fading of the dyes on the negative. If color negatives have been properly processed and then appropriately stored, they could have a useful life of 100 years. This time frame will be lessened by the typical household storage of negatives found in most American homes.

Safe storage materials include acid-free paper, polyester, triacetate, polypropylene, polyethylene, and Tyvek. These sleeves of negatives should then be stored as described above.

Unsafe materials for storing negatives are glassine envelopes, vinyl or other plastic sheets containing PVCs, non-acid free paper, kraft paper envelopes.

As mentioned several times, proper storage of prints is essential. The above types of plastics apply for prints as well. Archival album and scrapbooks are readily available today. Archival print sleeves are now available that have inserts to identify photographs. Also available are archival labels for slides, the back of pictures, etc. Do not write with ink on the back of photographs.

REMEMBER: Never do what you can't undo. The best way to identify prints on the back is with pencil, preferably on an archival label. Write the information on the label BEFORE attaching to the back of the photograph to prevent scoring the picture.

If you have important prints that you wish to preserve here are a few precautions to take in the use of photograph storage or tissue paper:

- Non-buffered (pH 7.0- 7.5) can be used for albumen, cyanotype, dye transfer, and color prints.
- Buffered paper (pH 8.0-8.5 with 2% calcium carbonate) can be used for storage of nitrate base film, B & W silver halide film and papers.
- Glassine is not recommended for long-term photographic storage.

If possible, store negatives in a separate location from the prints, like a bank safety deposit box. At the least, they should be stored in a fire-proof box, which can be found in many variety and office supply stores. Humidity can be controlled by keeping in an air conditioned room or by use of desiccants in the storage container or area. Photography archival supply companies like Light Impressions offer desiccant boxes that will easily take care of the humidity in these home safes.

COLOR NEGATIVES AND PRINTS

Color negatives differ from black and white negatives in that the color is achieved by dyes found on the emulsion side of the film. The major preservation problem with color film is its stability. The dyes on the negative, if not kept in proper conditions, will fade or change in quality. In addition, the prints may not be as stable as desired. Early color prints from the 1950s for example, may already show signs of fading or color change. The best preservation advice is to preserve the color negatives as best as possible and then also use only archival albums for the prints. In addition, if you have special color images you wish to preserve, you should have true black and white copies made

When your family has important events you wish to photograph, like 4 or 5 generation pictures, family reunions, etc., it is important for the survival of these images to have also taken black and white pictures in addition to our color ones. Future generations will be grateful that you did.

NOTE: Some film manufacturers like Kodak now sell a new form of black and white film that can be developed by the many 1-hour Photo shops. It is important to note that this film is on a color negative base (designated by CN after the number on the box) and, therefore, has the same stability problems as any other color film. When buying B & W film, buy the true B & W film and have it processed by a B & W lab. It may take a little more time and money, but down the road, it will be worth it.

HAZARDOUS NITRATE FILM AND NEGATIVES

If you have older film negatives made before 1951, you need to check the negatives very carefully. These older negatives may be on nitrate film, which is very combustible.

It is usually easy to determine if the film is nitrate. On the margin of the film negative it will state it is nitrate. If the margin has been trimmed off, nitrate film will also smell of nitric acid, especially if it is starting to deteriorate. The negatives may also be very brittle. The film base may also have turned yellowish or amber.

Film that should be checked includes the following:

- Size 135 roll film before 1938.
- Portrait and commercial sheet film before 1939.
- Aerial film before 1942.
- Film packs before 1949.
- Roll film in sizes 616, 620, etc. before 1950.
- Professional 35mm motion-picture film before 1951.

After the above stated dates for each type, the above film types were done on safety film. If you find these among your family collections, it is important that you properly care for them.

First, store nitrate negatives in the freezer after inserting each one in separate paper envelopes and the envelopes in moisture-proof containers. This will slow the deterioration of the negative even if none has been detected.

Second, find a qualified photographer who is willing to make new negatives (copy negatives) from the nitrate ones.

Third, once the new safe negatives have been made, handle the nitrates as you would any hazardous, highly combustible material, and dispose of the nitrate film. If you have only a few negatives, the safest way to dispose of these is through open burning, following, of course, your local fire regulations. **Do not use enclosed furnaces to burn these.** If, however, you have a large collection of nitrate negatives or film, it is advisable to contact a hazardous waste disposal company to properly and safely destroy the material.

A good source for more information on the care and storage of historic photographs and negatives is *Collection, Use, and Care of Historical Photographs* by Robert A. Weinstein and Larry Booth (Nashville: American Association for State and Local History, 1977).

DISPLAYING PHOTOGRAPHS

Some of us have inherited impressive collections of photographs or individual pieces. The natural inclination is to display these for all our visitors and family to see and enjoy. However, if these old photographs are on display they are in grave danger of deterioration and even destruction from fire, water damage and other environmental problems.

The biggest threat to preservation of the image is ultraviolet rays which are all around us. These can cause all photographs to fade. Another danger is acid that may be in the display materials like frames, especially those old wooden frames that may be original to the print.

So what do we do? Hide away those great family photographs in our archival boxes or fire-proof safes? The simple archival answer is yes. However, if you have a large format photograph or print, like I have of my great-grandparents just prior to their marriage, you may decide to display them. If you do, then do so in as safe a manner as possible.

First, have a true black and white negative made of the photograph for preservation purposes. Store it archivally and safely. Then have the photograph framed archivally—everything touching or surrounding the original should be acid-free. Use only acid free mat board, use acid-free paper to seal the back of the frame, and frame in a metal frame. In addition, you should use UV glass or plexiglass to protect the image. Do not allow the glass to come in contact with the photograph.

However, the best solution to displaying those great photographs is using a copy. Make a print from a photographic negative, or if you have a scanner, scan the image for the size you want to display. If the copy is actually a photograph, then frame it in the same manner as outlined above. A scanned print can be framed in a less expensive and non- archival way since you can always make another copy if you have stored the photograph in some computer format.

For larger collections, like a family album of photographs that we may want to share with relatives, then use the many archival scrapbook possibilities available today. Most companies like Light Impressions and 20th Century Plastics now carry archival album supplies. Some craft stores also carry scrapbook supplies. However, be sure the materials you are using are archivally safe. If you are going to the trouble to make an album for your children, then don't you want it to last as long as the originals have? It may take a little more time, effort and money, but your descendants will be very grateful.

COMPUTERS AND PHOTOGRAPHS

The technology we have today is truly amazing when compared to 20+ years ago when I first started researching my families and beginning my photograph collection. Everyday it seems there is some new development and our computers are out of date as soon as they come off the shelf and into our homes.

The latter point is the prime thing to remember about computers and our photographs: computer technology is changing daily; however, actual negative based photography has been around and virtually unchanged for over 150 years. We can still make prints from negatives that were made in the latter part of the 19th century. Ask yourself this question: will the computers one hundred years from now look like the ones we have today, and, even more importantly, able to read the disks, CD's, zip disks we make today? The answer is probably a resounding NO.

So what is the point? First, if you are reading this book, you are interested in preserving all of your photographs so your descendants will be able to enjoy them as much as you do today. That preservation is not via computers. SORRY, but if you put all your photographs on CD's, etc., your descendants may have to go to the Smithsonian to have the disks read instead of just opening an album and browsing through the family pictures in the comfort of their home.

Therefore, remember computers and their accessories are not the ways to preserve our photograph memories.

However, computers can be a valuable tool in genealogy and photography. What follows are a few comments on the uses of computer technology and photographs.

SCANNING—Many people may wonder about the harm scanning may do to old photographs. To be honest, since the technology is relatively recent, not enough information is available to be make guarantees. However, from what I have read in the literature, scanning will do less harm than exposing the photograph to daylight. The major precaution to take when scanning is to limit exposure to the scanner light. If for some reason, you plan to repeatedly scan a photograph, then use a photographic copy rather than the original.

Scanning photographs into our computer allows us to share photos through the internet with our relatives, put them on our web pages, or attempt to improve the quality of the original. The latter point is worthy of consideration for those images that are faded or damaged in some way. There are many photo editing software programs available. Talk to friends about the programs they use, read reviews on the net or in photograph magazines. One magazine that is helpful and easy to read is *PCPhoto* (Box 56380, Boulder, CO 80323-6380 or www.pcphotomag.com).

Many genealogy programs now are capable of incorporating scanned images. *FamilyTree Maker 7.0*, for example, allows users to directly scan photographs into the scrapbook feature. When purchasing or upgrading genealogy software, check for this feature, for it can save us time especially if one is planning to publish a family history. Family trees with photographs are also possible now as well as calendars dedicated to our own particular families. What fun!!

RECORDABLE CD

This compact storage format is great. Although this is a relatively new format, the potential is astounding. No one can guarantee the life of the material on a CD. I have read 50 years and beyond. If true, then this is indeed a preservation format to consider. The October 1999 issue of *PCPhoto* discussed this format in "For the Record: CD-Recordable and CD-ReWritable Drives are an Ideal Way to store and Preserve Images." The following statement was found about half way through the article:

> *The ideal long-term storage is a medium that's stable, as archival as possible and doesn't rely on a unique format to be read–that is, it **can be used on a variety of computers anywhere.*** [my boldface]

Therefore, again the question we need to ask ourselves is not if the CD will last, but will there be technology to read it? If we cannot say absolutely, then the CD may go the route of the 5" floppy. So it is important to archivally preserve our negatives and prints the old fashion way until we can guarantee the format **and** the technology will be always be there.

PHOTOGRAPH COMPUTER PRINTING

Today we can order our photographs on CD along with our regular prints. I have been doing that for my current family photographs. As I copy my old ones, I have been doing the same thing. We can also scan our photographs and save them on CD. The next issue then is the quality and lifespan of the prints we may make with the assistance of our laser or inkjet printers.

First, although the inkjet printers have come down in price, the photographic ink and paper is not inexpensive. This will probably change, just as we have seen other computer related prices fall. But at the moment, printing our own pictures is not a cheap way to go. Inkjet cartridges can break you, and the prices of color lasers is still fairly high for most home offices.

Another factor to consider is the lifespan of the paper and the ink we use to make the prints. At the moment, inkjet prints will not last more than a couple of years. Hewlett-Packard has improved the quality of their ink so that "Lightfastness" will probably be stable up to 3 years and "darkfastness" perhaps to 50 years.
The best way to keep inkjet prints is to keep them away from light exposure, but we will have to make new prints very quickly when compared to the old film format prints, even our color prints.

Archival print paper is available and even archival ink, but the latter may not be compatible with your printer or its driver. Be very careful about using third party ink cartridges in your printers for they may damage your printers.

From what I have read, printer and print supply manufacturers are aware of the demand for stable paper and inks that result in prints with a long lifespan like our old ones. Hopefully in the not too distant future we will be able to print archival prints at home. I am looking

forward to that day, but until then, it is still the old fashion way for me and my collection.
(See *PCPhoto*, November 1999, "Inkjet Papers," pp. 102-104.)

DIGITAL CAMERAS

This looks like the wave of the future to many people. It is quick and fun. With a digital camera you can quickly input your photos into your computer and the world beyond via the net. However. these cameras are very expensive for the average person.

Before you throw out your old 35mm camera, keep in mind that digital cameras are miniature computers. Computer chips can crash and files can be corrupted on the camera just like on your desktop. So once again I ask myself will the technology be there in the future? Too soon to tell for me to feel comfortable relying solely on digital cameras for my important family photographs.

Another factor is that the resolution or quality of digital prints has not quite equaled the 35mm film negative or print. It may be in the future but the best quality print is still from the 35mm negative.

If you want the latest in cameras, feel free to go digital but don't throw out your 35mm camera. Put real Black and White film in your 35mm camera to take those 5-generation shots or the other important family milestones pictures. Preserve the negatives and have fun with the digital.

SURFING THE NET

The worldwide web is vast information source available from our home computer. Once on the net we can find many helpful sites for computers and photography. Photographic and computer magazines have website with back issues of their magazines and additional articles not found in the hard copy issue.

Other sites are out there that might be of interest to you, even if you are not going to scan your photographs, etc. I have listed some of them below. They all usually have links to other sites of a similar nature. Have fun surfing!

Conservation Online
        palimset.stanford.edu.

American Museum of Photography
        www.photographmuseum.com

International Museum of Photography and Film
        www.eastman.org

Antique Photo Guide
        www.city-gallery.com

The Daguerreian Society
        www.daguerre.org

The American Photographic Society
        www.superexpo.com/APHS

The Photoforum Homepage
        www.rit.edu/~andpph/photoforum

Also check out the photographs at the Library of Congress website.

Archivally Copying Old Photographs

There are two ways to accomplish the archival copying of our old pictures when we do not have negatives in our possession. First, is using a professional photographer. Second, do it yourself.

USING THE PROFESSIONAL– This can be the best way to go

if one does not have many photographs to copy. However, if a large number of photographs are to be copied, then this can be a very expensive proposition.

If a state historical society or university archives is nearby, contact them to see if they do archival copy work for the public. If this is not possible, call around to the various photography studios regarding their archival copying procedures and costs. Inquire about the costs of just making the negative as well the costs of prints. Archival prints need to be done on rag or fiber paper, not resin-coated paper.

When using either a public institution or a professional photographer, one important detail to work out prior to commitment is who will own the negative. Many professionals consider all negatives their property, but some will hand over the negative for this type of work.

DO IT YOURSELF
What you will need:

 Single Lens Reflex adjustable 35mm camera.

True Black and White film Slow speed or fine grain film works best.

 A macro or close up lens will be needed to copy most photographs.

 A copy stand or tripod to steady the camera

A source of light for indoor shooting. Many portable copy stands come with 2 or 4 light attachments like the one shown here.

If you plan to do the printing as well, you will need rag or fiber paper and fresh chemicals.

My copy stand comes apart and will fit in a medium sized suitcase. This is ideal to take on genealogy trips to libraries, archives, or relatives' houses as I can make the copies onsite. When I plan to go on a research trip which may include access to photographs, I pack up my copy stand, check the stand's light bulbs, buy a number of rolls of B & W film, check my camera batteries and have a spare in the camera case. There is nothing more frustrating to get everything set up to take pictures and the bulbs have burnt out or the camera batteries are dead. When in a strange town, it is often time-consuming to find camera supplies, like batteries. Experiment at home with exposure times, etc., before going "on the road" to make copies. Shoot a couple of rolls of film–less expensive if you use color at first, and then work up to B & W film.

When copying photographs indoors, turn off all lights if possible and setup away from windows. This may not always be possible, but eliminating as much outside light as possible will make for a better copy. The lights should be at a 45 degree angle. Check for glare before shooting the picture. Adjust the lights to eliminate any glare. The lights can become very hot, so it is important to limit an original photograph's exposure to the heat of the lamps. Get organized and shoot copies as quickly as possible.

Since I do not have a darkroom, I send my film to a studio for processing. One-Hour labs do not process black and white film.

However, they should know of a studio for the developing and printing. Black and White is a little more expensive to have processed, but it is worth it. Once I see the proofs or initial prints, I can have any size made for my collection or to share with relatives.

If you are planning to make your own prints, it is important to educate yourself on archival printing from B & W film. Check with your state historical society for information on this, or contact Eastman Kodak for advice. Your local library may have information as well.

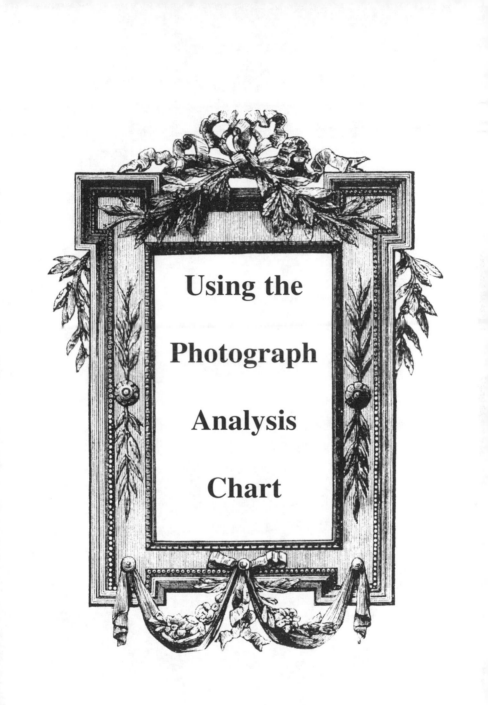

Using the

Photograph

Analysis

Chart

Using the Photograph Analysis Chart

If necessary, attach a photocopy of photograph to take to libraries, etc. when researching costumes, etc.

1. Identify photographic process

2. What photographer's information, if any, is found on photograph?

3. Briefly identify distinguishing fashion characteristics.

4. Note any other markings, props, etc. For example, can you date the furniture in the picture?

5. After filling in the dates' section, compare dates. Are they about the same period? Major differences may mean the photograph is a copy of an earlier format like a daguerreotype.

- Cabinet Card 1869-1920

- Fashion: tight skirt with pleated ruffle, small bustle, overskirt, lace jabot at neck. 1880s?

- Props/background: elaborate balustrade, fireplace

- Photographer: VanSickle, Springfield, Ohio–Checked *Ohio Photographers* dates for VanSickle --c 1881-1886

91

Photograph Analysis Chart

Name of Person(s) in Photograph:

_____

Photographic Process:
Daguerreotype (1840-1860)   _____   Size:_____   Type Case_____
Ambrotype (1851-1880   _____   Size: _____   Type Case:_____
Tintype (1853-1930s)   _____   Size: _____   Type Case:_____
Carte de Visite (1854-1885)   _____
Cabinet Card (1869-1920   _____   Tinted?_____
Other (Specify)_____

Photographer Information:
Name:_____
Studio Address: _____
Other markings/information?_____
Fashions:
Men: Lapels_____   Coat/Vest:_____
Cravat/ties _____   Pants: _____
Hats: _____   Hairstyle: _____
Facial Hair _____   Other: _____

Women: Skirt Style: _____   Bodice: _____
Collar/neckline _____   Head wear _____
Patterns: _____   Jewelry _____
Hairstyle: _____   Hats: _____

Children: Gender: M   F   Dress_____   Pants_____   Age?_____
Girls: Dress _____   Shoes/Stockings _____
Hairstyle _____   Hats: _____
Other _____
Boys: Pants (short/long) _____   Jacket style _____
Hats: _____   Stockings/shoes _____
Hairstyle _____   Other: _____

Other Items of Interest:
Background: _____
Props: _____
Markings on Image: _____
Compilation of Dates:
Type of Photograph_____   Photographer _____
Fashion _____   Other information dates _____
Approximate date of image: _____   Date of actual Photograph _____
(Note: If date of image and date of photograph do not match, the photograph could be a copy of an earlier format.)

Copyright 2000Diane Gagel

BIBLIOGRAPHY

Auer, Michele and Michel Auer, eds. *Photographers Encyclopedia International, 1839 to the Present.* 2 vols. Hermance, Switzerland: Editions Camera Obscura, 1985.

Baldwin, Gordon. *Looking at Photographs: A Guide to Technical Terms.* Malibu, CA: J. Paul Getty   Museum, 1991.

Bennett, Stuart. *Christie's Collectors Guides: How to Buy Photographs.* Oxford, England: Phaidon, 1987.

"Care and Storage of Color Slides." Brochure from *Light Impressions.*

Caring for Photographs.: Display, Storage, Restoration. NY: Life Library of Photography, Time Life Books, 1972.

Clark, Walter. *Caring for Photographs.* Vol. 17 of the Life Library of Photography. New York: Time-Life Books, 1972.

Broecker, William L., ed. *Encyclopedia of Photography.* New York: International Center of Photography; Crown, 1984.

Conrad, James H. "Copying Historical Photographs: Equipment and Methods." American Association for State and Local History Technical Leaflet 139.

Crawford, William. *The Keepers of the Light: A History & Working Guide to Early Photographic Processes.* Dobbs Ferry, NY: Morgan & Morgan, 1979.

Dalrymple, Priscilla Harris. *American Victorian Costumes in Early Photographs.* New York: Dover   Publications, Inc., 1991.

Davies, Thomas L. *Shoots: A Guide to Your Family's Photographic Heritage.* Danbury, NH: Addison House, 1977.

Eaton, George T. "Preservation, Deterioration, Restoration of Photographic Images. " *Library Quarterly* 40 (January 1970): 85-98.

----------------------. *Photographic Chemistry in Black and White and Color Photography.* 3rd Ed. Dobbs Ferry, NY: Morgan and Morgan, 1981.

Frisch-Ripley, Karen. *Unlocking the Secrets in Old Photographs.* Salt Lake City: Ancestry, 1991.

Gagel, Diane VanSkiver. *Ohio Photographers, 1839-1900.* Nevada City, CA: Carl Mautz Publishing, 1998.

-----------------------------."Historic Photography: Identification and Preservation." *Ancestry.* Vol. 14:6 (Nov/Dec 1996): 7-13.

-----------------------------. "Card and Paper Photographs, 1854-1900. *Ancestry.* Vol. 15:5 (Sept/Oct 1997): 13-17.

Hendricks, Klaus. "Preserving Photo Records: Materials, Problems and Methods of Restoration." *Industrial Photography* 27 (August 1978): 30.

Henisch, Heinz K. and Bridget A. Henisch. *The Photographic Experience, 1839-1914: Images and Attitudes.* 1994.
--. *The Painted Photograph 1839-1914: Origins, Techniques, Aspirations.* University Park, PA: Pennsylvania U. Press, 1996.

Hill, May Davis. "Hidden Stories in Your Photographs." *Family Heritage* June 1978: 86-94.

Horridge, Patricia, & Diane G. Smathers, Diane L. Vachon. "Dating Costumes: A Check List Method." *History News* 32 (Dec 1977): 327-339.

Johnson, William S. *Nineteenth Century Photography: An Annotated Bibliography.* Boston: Hall & Co., 1990.

Keefe, Jr., Laurence E. and Dennis Inch. *The Life of a Photograph: Archival Processing, Matting, Framing, and Storage.* Boston: Focal Press, 1984.

Kelbaugh, Ross J. *Introduction to Civil War Photography.* Gettysburg, PA: Thomas Publications, 1991.

Lawrence, John H. *Preservation Guide 2: Photographs.* New Orleans: The Historic New Orleans Collection, 1983.

Leisch, Juanita. *Who Wore What? Women's Wear 1861-1865.* Gettysburg, PA: Thomas Publications, 1995.

Miller, Ilene Chandler. *Preserving Family Keepsakes.* Yorba Linda, CA: Shumway Family History Services, 1995.

Newhall, Beaumont. *The Daguerreotype in America.* New York: New York Graphic Society, 1968.

Norris, Herbert and Oswald Curtis. *Nineteenth Century Costume and Fashion.* Mineola, NY: Dover Publications, 1998.

Ostroff, Eugene. "Preservation of photographs." *Photographic Journal* 107 (October 1967): 309-314.
--------------------. "Conserving and Restoring Photographic Collections." Washington: American Association of Museums, 1975.

Palmquist, Peter, ed. *Photographers: a Sourcebook for Historical Research.* Nevada City, CA: Carl Mautz, 2000.

Pohls, Robert. *Understanding Old Photographs.* Oxford, England: Robert Boyd Publications, 1995.

Rinhart, Floyd and Marion Rinhart. *American Daguerreian Art.* New York: Clarkson N. Potter, Inc., 1967.

Rosenblum, Naomi. *A History of Women Photographers.* NY: Abbeville Press, 1994.

Rudisill, Richard et al. *Photographers: A Sourcebook for Historical Research.* Brownsville, CA: Carl Mautz Publishing, 1991.

Severa, Joan L. *Dressed for the Photographer: Ordinary Americans and Fashion, 1840-1900.* Kent, OH: Kent State U. Press, 1995.

Shull, Wilma Sadler. *Photographing Your Heritage.* Salt Lake City: Ancestry, 1988.

Taft, Robert. *Photography and the American Scene: A Social History, 1839-1889.* New York: Dover Publications.

"Tips for Proper Negative Storage." Brochure from *Light Impressions.*

Ulseth, Hazel and Helen Shannon. *Victorian Fashions, 1890-1905.* Vol. II. Cumberland, MD: Hobby House Press.

Webster, Mary. "Frames for Photographs." *Victorian Homes* Spring 1991: 52-59.

Weinstein, Robert A. and Larry Booth. *Collection, Use, and Care of Historical Photographs.* Nashville, TN: American Association for State and Local History, 1977.

Welling, William. *Collector's Guide to Nineteenth Century Photographs.* New York: Collier Books.

Witkin, Lee D. and Barbara London. *The Photograph Collector's Guide.* Boston: New York Graphic Society, 1979.

Wood, John, ed. *America and the Daguerreotype.* Iowa City: U. of Iowa Press, 1991.

10/05